A Fall to Grace

*Bill,
May God open the doors for you He has opened for me*

MB

CAP'T MICHAEL BALL

A Fall to Grace

Trilogy Christian Publishers A Wholly Owned Subsidiary of Trinity Broadcasting Network

2442 Michelle Drive Tustin, CA 92780

Copyright © 2022 by Cap't Michael Ball

All Scripture quotations are taken from the Holy Bible, New International Version®, NIV®. Copyright © 1973, 1978, 1984, 2011 by Biblica, Inc.TM Used by permission of Zondervan. All rights reserved worldwide. www.zondervan.com. The "NIV" and "New International Version" are trademarks registered in the United States Patent and Trademark Office by Biblica, Inc.TM

No part of this book may be reproduced, stored in a retrieval system, or transmitted by any means without written permission from the author. All rights reserved. Printed in the USA.

Rights Department, 2442 Michelle Drive, Tustin, CA 92780.

Trilogy Christian Publishing/TBN and colophon are trademarks of Trinity Broadcasting Network.

Cover design by: Blair Cruz

For information about special discounts for bulk purchases, please contact Trilogy Christian Publishing.

Trilogy Disclaimer: The views and content expressed in this book are those of the author and may not necessarily reflect the views and doctrine of Trilogy Christian Publishing or the Trinity Broadcasting Network.

Manufactured in the United States of America

10 9 8 7 6 5 4 3 2 1

Library of Congress Cataloging-in-Publication Data is available.

ISBN: 979-8-88738-241-8

E-ISBN: 979-8-88738-242-5

Table of Contents

FOREWARD 1

INTRODUCTION 3

CHAPTER ONE: MY EARLY CHILDHOOD 5

CHAPTER TWO: LOSING MY INNOCENCE 13

CHAPTER THREE: LIFE ON MY OWN 19

CHAPTER FOUR: FISHING—A WAY OF LIFE..................................... 27

CHAPTER FIVE: COMMERCIAL SCALLOPING —THE BIG TIME 37

CHAPTER SIX: THE GIG WAS UP 57

CHAPTER SEVEN: STARTING OVER 69

CHAPTER EIGHT: LIFE GETS REAL 89

CHAPTER NINE: DARKEST BEFORE THE DAWN 95

CHAPTER TEN: NEVER TOO LATE FOR A NEW CAREER.......................... 101

CHAPTER ELEVEN: BLESSINGS, UPON BLESSINGS, UPON BLESSINGS........ 113

CHAPTER TWELVE: GRATEFUL 121

Foreward

Written by Lori Ball (my wife)

This book was written for the sole purpose of giving people hope. In my opinion, 2020 through 2021 were a couple of years that we won't soon forget. Our country was amid a pandemic, on the heels of a contentious election, and experiencing the abrupt end of a twenty-year-long war. Prejudice, hatred, and division were at an all-time high because of race, social injustice, and gender identity. It seemed there were protests and disagreements everywhere! During this time, Michael was home due to a shoulder injury and started writing this book because he realized that now more than ever, society needs hope. Inspiration. Encouragement. And grace.

This is a story of a regular boy from a small town in Maine who grew up to be a fisherman. He started with hopes and dreams, like any other kid. He played sports, hunted, fished, and went to school and church. He wanted to belong and be liked, and he looked up to his father. He was never wealthy but had everything he needed. But, early on in his childhood, things began to unravel for his parents, which took a direct toll on his life.

As the years went on, this smiling young boy became a young man, and as things continued to become more unmanageable in his parents' lives, they started to affect his life negatively. Leaving home as a teenager, he quit school and started drinking and using drugs. Then he would pull himself up out of the muck to only fall further down the next time. He almost didn't survive many of the situations that he went through; however, God was always there, watching and waiting. God always had a plan and a purpose for him.

God has a plan and a purpose for you too. Sometimes, when life is rough, we can think that God has left us. We think we are too far gone. This testimony confirms that we are never too far gone! God will never leave us or forsake us! The purpose of sharing this story is to give hope to one more person.

Introduction

I have written this book in the hope that I can reach those people who suffer from a lack of faith and who struggle with addiction issues. To know God is to know faith, no God, no faith... simple, right? Well, not so earlier in this ex-addict's life, but I'm here to tell you that anything is possible in life with a few simple things: God, a good recovery program, and a willingness to move forward through it all!

Chapter One:
My Early Childhood

At that time the disciples came to Jesus and asked, "Who,
then, is the greatest in the kingdom of heaven?" He called
a little child to him and placed the child among them. And
He said: "Truly I tell you, unless you change and become like
little children, you will never enter the kingdom of heaven.
Therefore, whoever takes the lowly position of this child is the
greatest in the kingdom of heaven. And whoever welcomes one
such child in my name welcomes me."

Matthew 18:1–5

My life started on October 16th, 1958, in the small seaside
town of Belfast, Maine, the same place my father was born. My
first memories aren't of Belfast because I was too young, but of
a place called Porter's Landing in South Freeport, Maine, which
was also on the coast. At that time, my life was full of adventure,
exploring the salt marshes of the landings, which was unique. My
parents rented the first floor of a house there, and the landlord
had a little girl my age, so it set the stage for my first crush. Of
course, I was only five or so.

A couple of years later, we moved to a place in the middle of
Maine called Andover. It was surrounded by mountains and forest
and was just a beautiful place. It was full of adventures to be experienced. My brother, Bob, was five years older than me. Bob was
born in New Jersey during my dad's deployment in the service.
My dad went overseas with his identical twin brother, Richard.
They served together touring Europe, fixing the communications
destroyed during World War II. When they were discharged, they

decided to move back to Maine. My mom and her best friend, Bea, had met the twins in New Milford, CT, when they were training to deploy, and they married the twins.

My mom had two sisters, and her parents came from Lithuania and Poland. They were hard-working and salt-of-the-earth people who raised a family that stuck together. This contrasted with my dad's family, which was really broken. The twins were given up at birth and my "real" grandfather, whom I had never met, asked his sister to raise them along with her son, Thornton. Uncle Thornton and my "grandmother" were all the relatives that I knew on that side of the family.

So, back to Andover. The twins were very close, and my uncle, Richard, had two children, David and Kathy, who were a little over five years older than me, the same as my older brother. I was the baby, and let me tell you: they weren't very kind to me. They left me in the woods, shot at me with the BB gun, and pretty much abused the crap out of me!

My dad was working for AT&T, and they were building a place on Black Mountain called Earth Station. This was a tracking station for the Cold War. I got to go to work with him occasionally to see the construction. It was so interesting! It was a huge dome that housed this big radar and these long "ray" guns that came out of the floor that could track Russian planes flying overhead. This was where a technical team, including my dad, participated in tracking the launch of the first communications satellite, which was called Telstar. I remember my dad got to sit in with Walter Cronkite and David Brinkley when the satellite was launched!

My dad was a supervisor, so he had a big crew working for him. Many of them were Micmac Indians, who became some of his best friends, and their kids were my best friends while we lived in Andover. At that time, life was simple and good, except for my dad's drinking, of which there was a lot. I started to notice that my dad had a very bad temper when drunk. He started to verbally abuse my mom, and it really scared me.

6 | A Fall to Grace

We had built a new home, and it was beautiful. I remember, at one point, we housed four members of the US Olympic Ski Team. Andover had lots of snow and mountains, so they came up to train in cross-country skiing and jumping. I was so impressed with this, and I started "training" with them. I won my first cross-country race, but then I decided to try ski-jumping without any training or supervision. On my first jump, I made an unbelievable jump, but the wind caught my ski tip before I landed, and it stuck into the snow, and I ended up with a compound fracture of my left leg. Because the location was so remote, other skiers had to get my mom. She climbed down the hill with one of those round metal saucers meant for sledding, put me on it, dragged me back up the hill, and drove me to Rumford, which was about thirty minutes away, to the emergency room! This was the first of many crazy stunts I was to partake in. It was early spring when I broke my leg, so come summer, I was still in a full cast and would go out with my friends. We would walk three to four miles, me on my crutches, go down to the river, and jump in. The cast would get soft and start unraveling by the time I got home. I had to get four or five replacement casts that summer! Yep, that's just how I rolled!

My uncle rented a beautiful farm on the ocean in Harpswell, Maine. We used to go spend time there, and one time I remember my two cousins and my brother, Bob, talking me into jumping off the roof. When I jumped, I landed on my head, which hit a rock, requiring stitches. This was typical for my summers!

My dad's family also owned about a hundred acres outside of Belfast, Maine, on which we had a small camp. The summer that I broke my leg, we all pitched in and built a nice large camp. We spent a few years enjoying the camp, and during hunting season, the twins and a bunch of dad's work crew came up to drink and hunt. Except for the heavy drinking and fighting at night, being at camp was a magical place in my life. As I got older, I got to go on a few of these hunting trips, most of which were filled with drinking, card games, and usually a trip to a local bar at night. I was

Chapter One: My Early Childhood | 7

about eight or nine at this time and realized something more was going on with these trips. Dad seemed to be a different person, and there were women involved. Mom used to question me when we got home, and then she would seem very angry. At that point, my brother had started doing drugs and was fighting with my dad, so things on the home front were starting to unravel.

Looking back at my childhood, I see I was always alone, trying to fit in. We would leave for camp right after school would let out in the summer. Dad was with his twin brother; Mom was with her best friend, Bea; Bob (my brother) and David and Cathy (my cousins) were together; and then there was me, the baby. I was always told to go and play. No wonder I have a hard time meeting and getting to know people.

After we were in Andover for a few years, my dad got a big promotion to supervise all the mountain top microwave installations in New England, and I believe this was a tipping point in his drinking. Soon after, we had to sell the house in Andover and move back to Freeport. We started renting this house on Summer Street, and once again, I had been yanked out of school and had to start over from scratch.

My dad was gone all week, so it was my mom, me, and my brother living together. My brother had started hanging out with some bad people. I just wanted to fit in, so I joined the little league and played third base for the LL Bean team, and I was pretty good. Of course, my dad was never there to watch me play. In one of our last games, I hit a fly ball deep to right field, and as I was rounding first base, I tripped, breaking my left arm, and I was off to get another cast! This ended my chances of making the All-Star team, but I did get an autographed ball by the whole team. Unfortunately, the doctor did not set my arm right, and I had to have corrective surgery later, which prolonged my recovery by at least six more months.

During my recovery, I used to get on my bike and ride to

8 | A Fall to Grace

South Freeport's Harraseeket Marina and sit on the dock to fish for mackerel. This is where I fell in love with the ocean. I could catch a ton of fish! It was about a ten-mile round trip bike ride from home to the dock and back again. I kept in shape while riding with one hand and holding my fishing pole with the broken one. In those days, I would be gone all day, and no one worried about me!

I made a few friends who lived on the same street as we did. My mom was a faithful Catholic, so I did my First Communion and confirmation and chose one of these friends' names as my middle name, which was part of the custom of confirmation. This was about the extent of my faith in God at that point! However, I think it was my mom's faith that was really holding her from leaving my dad, as things in their marriage were really getting out of control. My dad had traded beer for whiskey and always had a half gallon on the counter. He was really getting verbally abusive toward my mom, so much so that she used to tell me that some-day we were going to "pack up and leave the jerk!" When he was sober, he was an awesome person. One year he bought my brother a Chevelle SS! My brother abused that privilege, and I still don't know what ever happened to that car!

So, with my dad really going off the rails, my brother started getting arrested for petty drug offenses, and the cops started showing up at our house on a regular basis. I remember that one time he brought this girl into our home, and she was a runaway or something. Well, the cops showed up and searched the house and found her under Bob's bed. What a crazy time! Dad came home and kicked Bob out of the house! Just another day at the Ball residence!

Another time Bob and his cohorts ripped off a local drug-store. He was in his room, and I walked in to find him with a plate full of pills. He instantly grabbed me and said if I ever told anyone about it, he would hold me down and shoot me up with the drugs! I think this is the point I said to myself, "I will never ever drink or do drugs...ever!" Famous last words!

The town of Freeport was turning on us because of my brother and his friends' campaign of terror. My friends at school stopped wanting my company, and whispers were in the air about our family's dysfunction. So, we did what we did best and packed up and left the quaint town of Freeport for a small fishing village on the Midcoast of Maine.

Michael fishing with broken arm

Project Telstar Andover ME

Michael and Bob Andover ME

Chapter One: My Early Childhood | 11

Chapter Two:
Losing My Innocence

"Watch and pray so that you will not fall into temptation.
The spirit is willing, but the flesh is weak."
Matthew 26:41

From here on, I won't use the real names of people or places so that I don't ruin anyone's reputation!

We rented this huge house in the middle of the fishing village with a view of the ocean. The house had five bedrooms and a large yard. By then, my brother was gone, so it was just the three of us, and realistically, because my dad was away at work all week long, it was just my mother and me.

The village was small and beautiful, with most of the people earning a living lobster fishing. People were steeped in the heritage and lineage of generations of fishermen. I surely wasn't one of them, so I was considered an outsider. I started making friends, though, and I started attending a small school down on the peninsula. I joined the baseball team and started to fit in.

The people we rented the house from came up in the summer from New Jersey and moved back into the house. So, my dad bought a camper, and we headed to a campsite in Winslow State Park, located on the ocean. My uncle gave me a sixteen-foot boat with an outboard on it, and I bought seven wooden lobster traps and started fishing them out in the bay around Crab Island. It was a great summer filled with catching very few lobsters and lots of mackerel. Today, I know that the other fishermen were hauling my traps, leaving the doors open, and taking my lobsters to discourage me from fishing in their area. This is how lobstering is, very territorial with invisible lines passed down through the generations. But I was bitten by the fishing bug and was determined to keep fishing wherever I landed!

We got back to the main house in the fishing village in the fall, and I started hanging out with some of the kids from the village, and they took me in. This is where I was introduced to pot and beer against my better judgment. I felt it was the only way to fit in. I was in eighth grade, and my whole world seemed to be changing. All I thought about was hanging out with my friends, getting high, chasing girls, and being as rebellious as I could be. My grades went to almost failing, and school was really starting to be a drag. I lived for my after-school activities with my new friends, smoking pot and dreaming of setting lobster pots. I got through eighth grade by the skin of my teeth! By summer, Dad decided to camp at a local campsite, which was awesome for me. That spring/summer, I got to set my first lobster pots in the area!

As school let out, some of my friends would live on an island about a mile offshore, which was owned by the dad of one of my friends. It had a small camp on it with a wharf, and I was invited to stay with the boys. This was like a dream come true, away from parents and fishing for lobsters. How cool was that? We also traveled over to the next town, where a bunch of young guys lived, and we played them in softball and hockey and just had good competitive fun. I made lifelong friends!

When we were staying on the island, we used to take our boats across the bay to an old granite quarry and take baths. There were quarries all over the place with crystal clear water in them. They had huge cliffs to jump off and many ledges to party on. There were a few islands that were inhabited, and we used to go back and forth to visit them. I guess, way back, the settlers had to live on the islands because they feared Indian attacks.

During this first summer of living on the island, my dad got

14 | A Fall to Grace

another huge promotion, and his drinking really started to affect his job and home life. But I just had the most magical summer of my life, smoking pot and drinking all that I wanted. I also had sex for the first time and made the decision I would never leave that life.

We moved back into the huge house in the fall, and I started high school, and I just hated it. Most of my friends went to another school and were older than I was, plus home life was very toxic. I remember one night, my parents were really fighting, and my mom accused my dad of having an affair. He was really drunk and was being abusive. He decided he was leaving, and it freaked me out, so I grabbed him and begged him to stay. He did stay, but nothing changed.

My mom's family lived in New Milford, CT. Gramps was an upholsterer, and my grandma was a homemaker. Early on, we visited them every summer for a week, and I got to play with my cousins. This was great fun, but as my dad's drinking got worse, we stopped going, so my aunts would come and visit us. My dad just hated this and would get drunk and argue with them until he literally drove them away. This used to hurt my mom so much, but she was a faithful Catholic spouse and continued to stand by his side. To this day, the wedge that he drove between our families is still there. I am working on getting back together with that side of the family, and with God's help, it will happen. As for Dad's side, they won't even talk to me, and I've tried over and over to make amends to no avail.

About that time, starting high school, I crossed the line from using drugs to get high and have fun to an obsession to stay high. The one thing I had going for myself was an unbelievable work ethic, and that was how I fueled the fire of my addiction from that point on.

My dad decided to quit his job, and that sent my family into a tailspin. We found ourselves broke, so Dad started selling things to pay the bills. He sold the camper, paid most of our rent, and started looking for a job, but his drinking was out of control, and my mom was really depressed. That next spring, we moved into a small cottage on the water with no running water and, yup, you guessed it, an outhouse! Because we moved across town, I was going to be able to switch schools, and that was awesome because I would now be going to school with my friends, but I was disappointed with my dad. I guess you could say I was embarrassed by him losing everything.

I made it through freshman year with Cs, and so then another summer started. This time a friend of mine fished off another island, and there was a small shack that he was living in, and he invited me to stay with him. So, we bought a small plastic battery-operated record player and some Aerosmith and Bob Dylan albums and proceeded to smoke copious amounts of pot and haul our lobster traps every day. For our food and supplies, we would go to a store on the main island called the Island Store. We had friends working there, so that is where we did our shopping. We would wear hip boots, pull them up and fill them with loaves of bread and jars of mayonnaise for lobster sandwiches, maybe a few boxes of Pop-Tarts for breakfast, and off we would go, barely able to walk out the door! When we weren't "shopping," we would sit at the picnic table in the store next to the wine rack and drink the wine. We thought we were pirates!

We started doing hard drugs about this time—acid, speed, and this thing called angel dust. I still don't know what it was, but it whacked you out. One time there was going to be this big weekend party on this island twenty miles offshore, so a bunch of us got in a sixteen-foot outboard boat and headed offshore to the party. As I remember, we got about halfway there, and we realized we were so high we didn't know where we were. So, we pulled up to a bell buoy and hung off it until we sobered up and continued our way to the party. Why we never died doing things like that just blows my mind now. It had to be God!

Another adventure we used to go on was to get someone to buy

16 | A Fall to Grace

us a couple of cases of beer and then go to the island. From there, we would get in a rowboat or two and row to the local campsite, where we could find a few girls that would take a nice scenic row back to the island to drink a few beers with us. Now I know why I never gained any weight when I was young—I was always active!

As the summer faded, we were coming off the island to start school, and this was hard for me when living in a house with no running water. I had to take sponge baths, and I was so embarrassed by our new poverty status. Crazy now when I look back and understand my parents were just trying to do the best they could! My dad tried a few times to make a living by himself as a boat owner but just didn't have the capital to get set up right. I remember one night we were getting this bad nor'easter, and he had to save his boat. He and my brother went out and brought it around the island to the leeward side. They almost died that night—it was a crazy stunt! They made it, but he ended up losing the boat to the bank, and he decided to go sternman or deckhand on a few of the boats from other towns.

Most of my friends were on this program in school that allowed them to leave at noon and go lobstering for credits to graduate. So, I would just leave with them (even though I wasn't eligible for the program) and go sternman or haul my own traps. This didn't last very long, and after a few months, I got suspended for a couple of weeks. When I went back to school, I got into a screaming match with the principal and quit school for good. I was fourteen years old at that time. My mother was just heartbroken, something I could never make up to her. Today I regret quitting because of no high school reunions, just a GED to show at a job interview. When my dad found out, we got into a fistfight, and I walked out of the house for good. At that point, I pretty much became homeless.

Chapter Two: Losing My Innocence | 17

Michael's First Boat

Chapter Three:
Life On My Own

The Spirit clearly says that in later times some
will abandon the faith and follow deceiving
spirits and things taught by demons.

1 Timothy 4:1

I started sleeping on my friends' couches and working on
deck with the dad of one of my friends. It's funny nobody ever
said, "Maybe you should finish school." They just wanted to take
advantage of my work ethic. My friends and I pretty much just
pooled our money together to buy pot and food as we partied the
winter away. As summer rolled around, we headed back to the
islands to fish and smoke pot; it seemed like a dream. Just sitting
on the wharf watching the tide go in and out.

I was also working as a sternman with one of my friends
whose father had just given him a beautiful thirty-four-foot
wooden boat for graduation. I always said this friend could catch
a lobster in his bathtub—he just had a gift. In order to go lobstering in a certain territory or berth, you had to own your own land,
or your family had to lobster, and you were born into the business. Well, my friend decided he wanted to fish off one of the big
islands near our village. He bought a large, beautiful house out on
this island so he could fish there. The problem was the islanders
didn't want him out there for several reasons. So, one really foggy
morning, as we were rowing out to his boat, I thought, *We should
be at the boat by now*, and eventually, we saw an antenna sticking
out of the water. Someone had cut the hoses on the engine and
sunk his boat! Then a few days later, as we were fixing the boat,

someone burned down his house! My friend flew out to the island and got into a fight with a guy he thought burned down his house. He stabbed him and almost killed him. He got arrested, and off to prison he went. I ended up taking up his gear for him with his boat. It was going to be a while before he would get out of prison, so that's when I decided to buy a boat and really start fishing for myself. In the spring of 1976, I bought a thirty-foot Beals Island boat with a 353 GM engine in it. I bought it off a guy from Monhegan Island for about $6,500. Somehow, I got a loan for it, and I was so proud of this boat!

Then came the summer of cocaine. I set my traps with my new boat and was working really hard catching the spring run of lobsters. I was taking one to two of my younger friends out fishing with me and getting good catches. The boat was in pretty good shape, but it was an old wooden boat that leaked. I was fishing about ten miles offshore, and all my bilge pumps were always pumping water. I can't believe that with the weather we were fishing in, it never sank. Anyway, I started snorting coke at a few parties and fell in love with it from the start. When I was high on coke and pot, I could put in long days hauling traps. What I didn't realize was that I was an addict. Addiction runs in my family. Gramps died of liver failure due to drinking, my dad and his twin brother were alcoholics, and my brother was an addict, so I really had no chance once I started down that road.

That fall, a few of us had rented a couple of cottages on the shore and kept fishing until winter set in. Then we usually just partied through the worst of it. But that winter, a few of us decided to fly to Jamaica and check it out. So, three of my friends and I bought tickets, drove to Logan Airport in a snowstorm, boarded the plane, and were on our way. We landed in Montego Bay and found a guy in a van willing to give us a ride to Negril. We started heading toward Negril and had to stop every twenty to thirty miles and add water to the coolant. We ended up in the mountains, called the Cockpit Country, and stopped by the house

20 | A Fall to Grace

of one of his friends to get some pot. This dude was all anti-British, and we found out people were rioting in Kingston. This guy really hated the Crown. After partying with him, we all ended up agreeing about the British! We left that afternoon and went through Ocho Rios and got to Negril late that night. We rented a room so we could rest, and around 3 AM, somebody pulled up in front of our room and started beeping their horn. We opened the door, and this guy was standing there with a huge pan full of hash oil. We thought we were in heaven. Next, we rented a grass hut on the beach for $3 a night. It was called Miss Gloria's Sunset Cottages. We exchanged our cash through this dude called Bongo and had all kinds of people bringing us all kinds of drugs. We started drinking "shroom" tea, and let me tell you: it was quite a trip. We had such a fun time tripping and drinking Red Stripe beer. We ate lots of fruit, and the only soda we could buy was banana soda. It was nasty, but we drank it anyway. Negril only had one store back then, so we weren't too picky about food. We went to this one restaurant, and it had this huge speaker in the corner blasting Frank Sinatra and reggae songs. We stayed there for ten days and spent every penny we had. When we got back to Montego Bay, we went to this actual treehouse bar, which was twenty feet in a tree with a one-man band, where we drank lots of rum drinks. I had never experienced anything like this! Needless to say, we all passed out on the flight back to the USA.

Early next spring, as we were partying at a friend's cottage, he introduced us to this guy from New Hampshire. This guy asked us if we would be interested in bringing in a big load of pot from Colombia. We were all tripping, so of course, we said yes, and that is how I got introduced to smuggling. We started meeting with these guys and planning out where to pick up the bales off two of their sailboats, where to unload the stuff, and so on. It kind of seemed like a dream, and I had no clue what I was getting into and how it would change my life. We decided to pick up the pot on the backside of a cluster of islands not far offshore and bring it

Chapter Three: Life On My Own | 21

into a local private dock. We would place a bunch of lookouts all over the main roads to keep an eye on the local police department. They even gave us a small speed boat to check out locations. We also had one crew member on the only Coast Guard planes paid off so the boats could get to our spot.

It seemed like forever, but the day finally came, and I've got to tell you, I was scared to death! I was just hoping that my boat wouldn't break down. We went out around midnight, and it was thick with fog. We had three lobster boats. When we got out to the sailboats that were anchored up, I pulled my boat beside one of them and started throwing bales of pot on board. I filled the engine room full, then started stacking them like traps on deck. I was second to load, and I probably put around 6–7,000 pounds on my boat. When we got the third boat loaded, we headed out, and let me tell you: I was so nervous and so wide awake! We made it back to the dock and could only unload one boat at a time. So, we had to wait out on a mooring while the first boat was unloaded. One thing we had going for us was the thickness of the fog, which helped because there were houses right on the shore next to us. As we were unloading, we decided to throw at least ten to fifteen bales under the dock in case the dealers ripped us off. Each bale weighed between forty to fifty pounds. After we unloaded our boats, we filled two huge Ryder trucks and finished around 3 AM.

The time was critical because this was a working dock, and the fishermen would be coming down to go fishing around 4:30 AM. We got the trucks out of there and cleaned up what we could, put the boats on the moorings, and I can't explain to you the relief I felt. I was in tears and high-fiving everyone because we had gotten it done! A couple of hours later, a few of us went down to the dock, and there was pot everywhere from some of the ripped bales! We swept up at least two to three pounds off the wharf, plus we took the bales we had thrown under the dock and put them in a container on the dock. I can only speak for myself, but after this, I felt invincible. The song "Smuggler's Blues" had just come out on

22 | A Fall to Grace

the radio, and it just fit what we had done!

A few days before we made the run, I had met this girl in a local watering hole. She was beautiful and had a hot car. I was way over my head with this one! That morning after the run, she showed up at a trailer we were all gathered at, and so she became part of our group. We all had nicknames, and they had given me the name Kiddo because I was one of the youngest guys in our clan.

The money guys from New Hampshire had explained that if we wanted to keep doing these runs and not get caught, we had to keep a low profile, meaning no cash and flash. We were just a bunch of young men with old trucks and old boats trying to make a living, and this really changed everything. They left us some money, but the big payout would come in a few weeks, so we all went back to our regular schedule of hauling traps and partying at night.

We finally got the call to go and pick up some cash. My friend and I headed to New Hampshire to the "big" guy's house. When we got there, it was a huge, beautiful place, and we went inside, and he handed us a small case, and it contained $250,000! The most money I had ever seen at one time! This was crazy! We left, and for most of the ride home, we were mainly looking in the rearview mirror for the cops. We made it home and divided the money up. This started a drug-induced wild summer with this girl I had basically just met.

This girl was staying in a place in Rockport, ME. This was where the upper class lived, and the only time my buddies and I ever went there was to get drunk and fight, which we did often. We used to go to this bar called Mr. Kites, and even though we were mostly underage, we got served. Back then, the drinking age was eighteen, so we were really young! Anyway, I started staying with this girl who had just broken up with this rich kid who had this beautiful black Pontiac Trans Am. Me? I had an old boat and an old beat-up Chevy, so I couldn't understand what she saw in me. Obviously, my work was cut out for me. I had to impress her!

Chapter Three: Life On My Own | 23

I had one of my friends drive me up to Augusta Pontiac, and with a lunch bag full of cash, I drove off the lot with a white Pontiac Formula with T-tops and a four-speed stick shift. Yup, I was now a race car driver, or so I thought! I bought an unreal stereo and some big tires and rims, jacked up the back, and it was one sweet ride. I'm not sure if I ever impressed her, but it was fun while it lasted!

Now, most of my other Cocaine Cowboys, as we were dubbed by the older fishermen, were a little more sensible with their money. Some bought land, better boats, or built houses. Not me; I got in my new ride with my girl and a local drug dealer and drove to Massachusetts and picked up half a pound of coke. On our way home, we stopped at a hotel in Portland for the night. I guess this drug dealer had told someone of our journey, and that night the T-top was pried off my car, and someone went through everything looking for the coke. They even left a couple of rolled-up hundred-dollar bills on the seat. I guess this was when I decided I could not trust anyone and became very paranoid.

Soon everything started to unravel. The dealer, who was supposed to make me $10,000 on this coke, started snorting it and had it cut so bad that it wasn't any good. I was turning into a real trainwreck and had gotten so paranoid that I ended up on the lawn of one of my best friends, pointing a gun at him. Thank God I didn't pull the trigger. At some point, I had proposed to this girl, but I didn't know that she was also seeing her ex on the side. Most of my friends were starting to give up on me because I was going down a bad road, and I was becoming impossible to be around.

My parents had finally moved out of the cottage on the water and into a small house in town with running water, but I seldom ever visited them. The friend who was planning the next drug run had voted me out of any future deals, so when I ran out of money, which only took about six months, I was done. My boat got repossessed, my car got repossessed, and I got kicked out of a cottage that I was renting for lack of payment. My fiancée left me as soon as the money ran out. I remember just sitting on the shore,

24 | A Fall to Grace

wondering what had just happened. So, I got on a bus headed for Portland to look for a job on a boat. As I was walking the docks, I had a brief glance at what had just happened in my life. I failed and quit my dream. What I didn't know was that God had a hand in this, and it was all in the plan that He had for me.

Michael lobstering with wooden traps

Chapter Four:
Fishing - A Way Of Life

What good is it for someone to gain the whole
world, yet forfeit their soul?

Mark 8:36

It only took me a few hours to find a job. I was hired as an
engineer/deckhand to the sword-fishing boat Tiki 14. It was a
boat out of Panama City, FL, with a legend of a captain named
Tommy Martin, who lived in South Portland, ME. I had never
been longlining before and had lied about my mechanical abili-
ties, but I could learn on the fly, and I sure did! Our first trip was
out on Georges Bank, and it was so cool. When you get into the
Gulf Stream, there are so many creatures and fish everywhere.
There were four of us on the boat: Captain Tommy; Bob, who was
a Marine, golden glove boxer, and full-blooded Indian; Bill, who
was a middle-aged guy from Portland; and me, the youngest.

We would set our gear out at dusk and haul it in the early
morning. We ran forty miles of longline with 2,000 hooks that
we snapped on. It was quite an operation. We had a hug reel that
held the line, and the line went to a small stainless ring welded on
the stern ahead of a bait table. We would thread the line through
the ring, tie a radio buoy to it, and throw the buoy overboard as
the boat was going forward. Then Bob would bait the hooks, snap
them on the line, and throw them overboard. After every mile of
line, we would clip on a radar-reflective buoy and throw that overboard until we were done. Then we would wait until morning and
haul it back the same way in reverse but off the side of the boat.
Tom would stand up on the top of the boat and steer the boat

toward the high-flyers and buoys. We would unsnap the hooks as they came aboard. You could usually see a fish coming, and Tom would yell, "Fish!" Then we would slow down and gaff it aboard. We also had a large gaff on a winch for the big ones. I would clean the fish and send them down into the fish hole to be iced.

Our trips lasted from fourteen to twenty-eight days, and at this point, we were docking in Portland, ME. The cool thing about this job was that, come September, we would start fishing south and end up in the Gulf of Mexico for the winter. As summer faded and the fall winds kicked in, we filled the boat with fuel, food, and ice, and off we headed south. We got down as far as Frying Pan Shoal, which is off North Carolina, and set our gear. We caught a few swords and a whole bunch of hammerhead sharks. The first morning when we started to haul, there was a bunch of flying fish on deck. They were interesting to watch as they came off the top of the waves and glided along. It kind of makes you wonder why God would put wings on fish.

We pulled into Cape Canaveral to sell and get provisions. This is truly a unique port because it has a traffic light that tells you if the port is closed due to a rocket launch. I had brought a lobster trap with me, so I was curious as to what I could catch. I threw it overboard in the harbor and let it soak for an hour or so, then pulled it up, and to my surprise, it was full of colorful fish, which I gave to a fisherman fishing off the dock.

We left Port Canaveral and headed south, and just off the shore at Miami, we set our gear out again but didn't catch much. This whole experience was crazy for this Maine boy to be fishing off Miami. I just loved the show *Miami Vice* back in the day! My head was starting to clear up a bit; I guess this was my rehab, or as I called it, "seahab." We did have some beer and a little pot, but no hard drugs; thank You, Jesus! We went around Key West, and we always had a bunch of dolphins, turtles, and flying fish around us. The water was turquoise blue, and the weather was warm—it was just like a dream. I thought that the first sailors to sail those waters must have been so impressed!

28 | A Fall to Grace

We headed all the way up the West Coast of Florida to Panama City and docked the boat. This, for sure, wasn't Miami, but it was still cool! It's a big military town, and there was a jet in the middle of town. It was way different than Maine—the bars were in the back of package stores, and I started drinking with some real redneck hometown boys. We made four trips out of this place. We were doing okay, making $1,500–2,000 a trip, but we would stay in for two weeks. I would stay on the boat and be broke by the time we sailed again. I would call home occasionally, but I even stayed away through Christmas. This was the first time I hadn't been home, so it was a lonely and sad day for me, but I got drunk, and it passed.

The end of April rolled around, and we headed back up north. We were heading in the direction in which the Gulf Stream flowed, so we made really good time. We stopped in Cape Canaveral, then headed to Portland, Maine, to get ready for the summer season on Georges Bank. Somewhere along the way home, the owner of the boat and Captain Tommy got into a spat, and he quit the boat as we docked in Portland. He said he was going to get another boat called the Sea Harvester.

When I got off the boat in Portland, I took a bus to Rockland and went to my parents' new home. It was small but nice, and it was really good to see my mom. Dad was still drinking and doing a bunch of odd jobs. My mom had gotten a job at the local hospital, and together, they were starting to get on their feet again. I visited a few friends but felt like an outsider, so I waited for the call from Captain Tommy, which came in a couple of weeks; so I headed to Portland, and we sailed to the northern edge of Georges Bank. This boat was smaller, older, and wooden—not steel, so I was not as confident in this floating tub. We did okay the first trip; then Captain Tommy told us we were going to the Grand Banks off Newfoundland next trip. I was excited and a little scared because it was a very long trip.

We sailed out of Portland and got as far as Sable Island and

Chapter Four: Fishing—A Way Of Life | 29

hit some weather, so we put into the leeward side of the island and anchored up. Sable Island off Nova Scotia is an island that has had around 200–300 shipwrecks and has wild horses on it from some of these wrecks. I'm sure many lives have been lost there, so it was really unnerving to be there. It just didn't feel right, and I was glad to leave it after the storm. Before we got to the tail of the Grand Banks, we went over where the Titanic went down, and I got to pray for those lost souls. We fished a few days on the tail, then headed into St. John's, Newfoundland, to unload and restock our supplies.

St. John's is probably the most picturesque port I have ever been to. It has huge cliffs on each side as you go into it, and it looks like a natural harbor of rock walls. So beautiful. We tied up at the fish company but had to wait for customs to clear us before we could step off the boat. There were all kinds of fishing boats there, both big and small. As I was cleaning the boat, the crew from a Portuguese trawler stopped and asked me if I had any extra hooks. It was a strange request, but I gave them a few, and they invited me to check out their ship. I went aboard, and it was about 500 feet long, and it was a factory trawler, meaning that they processed all they caught. Many of the fishermen brought their wives with them because they would be away from home for up to a year! They wanted to take the hooks home so they could fish for food. I guess their wages weren't very good, which made me very grateful for being an American.

The main street in St. John's had at least one hundred bars on it, and they drank Newfoundland Screech and Golden Glow, of which I drank lots of and pretty much lost two days. I can't tell you how hungover I was on sailing day, but it was bad!

Captain Tommy decided to steam up to the Flemish Cap, and if you saw the movie *The Perfect Storm*, this is where they were. It's halfway to the Azore Islands. Going up there in this old wooden boat was crazy, to say the least, but off we went, fishing our way to Africa. It was surreal to be that far from home on the water, but I

30 | A Fall to Grace

kept occupied trying to keep the engines running and the pumps pumping so we wouldn't sink!

When we finally got up to the Flemish Cap, we had some great fishing, but there was a big storm coming, and we had to cut the trip short and beat feet for St. John's again. It took us four days to get there, and the weather had turned nasty. We took a beating the last couple of days. I was glad to put my feet on dry land. We stayed in port for four days and didn't unload our fish. On the last day we were there, Captain Tommy decided to transfer a bunch of fish off to another boat and take them with our catch back to Portland. This was welcome news for the rest of us on the boat. I think the captain realized that a small old wooden boat this far from home was foolish, so we headed back to Portland. It took us six days, and we put into New Bedford, MA, to unload the fish. I guess it wasn't on the up and up, if you know what I mean. I know this because it took three years for me to get paid for this trip!

One thing I've got to say about what I saw in St. John's was the number of churches. I feel that back in the day, God was a huge part of the fishing industry, and people used to have their boats blessed, and there was always prayer before every trip. We have lost that in America but in Newfoundland, it's still part of the fabric of their lives, and I can only hope that we Americans can get back to prayer again.

We steamed to Portland to get ready for one more trip to Georges Bank, then started our journey south to the Gulf. After we tied up, I went home to check on my mom because she had been diagnosed with breast cancer and had to have a mastectomy. When I got home, she was doing chemo and looked really sick. Her dad (my grandfather) had passed away, and her mother was sick also. Again, I had not been there to support her, and Dad was still drinking, but something had changed in him. He didn't look well, either. As for me, I just wanted to leave and not deal with it, as any good drug addict would.

Chapter Four: Fishing—A Way Of Life | 31

I stayed for a week and then got the call to head back to Portland, so I got on the bus and left both parents, who really needed my help. But, at this point in my life, it was all about me. We sailed two days later for a short trip of fourteen days. We did okay and headed to the dock, took our fish out, and got ready to head south for the winter. I went home for a couple more days to say goodbye to my parents for the winter. I left their house feeling that I should not go, but I was broke, so in my mind, I needed to go. We left Portland and fished our way down to Cape Canaveral, went in, packed our fish out, got our provisions, and left.

We didn't go to Panama City this time. We started fishing out of Fort Myers, which was a nicer place to dock the boat, and it is where I found out about Quaaludes or, as we called them, gorilla biscuits. Take two "714s" and a few beers, and you would be in a blackout for twenty-four hours. One time, I had taken a couple of these and drank a beer, and was walking across the Marco Island bridge; when I woke up, I was in an ambulance. I guess they had hit me with some Narcan or something because it woke me up fast. They said I had no pulse and would have died, one of many times this happened to me from here on out. Anyway, I refused medical treatment, and they let me out, so I headed to the bar... that is where my thinking was at.

We made a couple more trips out of Fort Myers, but we weren't doing very well, only catching a lot of small fish. We weren't getting paid very often, so as Christmas rolled around, the crew wanted to go home, and the owner gave us a $100 draw on our pay, so I decided to quit. That was the end of my sword fishing adventure. The other two guys quit also, and we bought bus tickets to Maine. We got a room and planned to leave the next day. Well, I wanted to get a tattoo before we left, so I went down to a studio and got some ink. Wouldn't you know it, the place gets raided by the ATF. I guess they were selling guns or something out of the back. I got cuffed, and they checked me out and let me go. Man, I was so done with Florida at that point!

32 | A Fall to Grace

We got on the bus the next morning, and off we went. We had brought a few bottles of Jack with us, and by the time we got to South Carolina, we were really drunk, and the bus driver kicked us off the bus until we sobered up. We passed out in some bus station in South Carolina and slept it off. We finally made it to Maine. It took two to three days, but it was nice to be home. I just wasn't sure what I would do for work.

My grandma had passed away, so Mom, Dad, and I traveled to Connecticut for the funeral. In the will, my mom's parents gave her a house in St. Petersburg, FL. This was a small place, but maybe they could get back on their feet. I got to see my cousins, and everything was good for a minute. We traveled back home, and I started looking for a job.

A few friends were working on a scallop boat out of Virginia, so I went down with them and got a job. We were fishing out of Portsmouth, RI, which is where America's Cup sailboat races were being held, so the place was mobbed. This was where I first used a needle to shoot up dope, and I instantly fell in love with it! We were making some okay money on the boat, but the captain and mate were really sketchy.

Scalloping is done with big steel frame drags. They measure anywhere from eleven feet to fifteen feet across the top. We had a bag of steel rings put together with links, and these were fastened to the steel frame with shackles. We also had a sweep chain attached to the bag and frame, a bunch of chains attached to the sweep and frame to keep the big rocks out, and on the top of the bag, there was a twine top made out of poly twine. We would tow a drag off each side of the boat with wire attached to big winches and to a bull ring on the bail of the drag. We had gallows or big steel frames on the stern or sides of the boat to take the strain of towing. We would haul back these drags every thirty to sixty minutes, pick them up and dump them out on the deck, set them back over, and then the crew would pick through the pile, putting the scallops in baskets and shoveling the rest back overboard. Then

Chapter Four: Fishing—A Way Of Life | 33

we would dump the baskets of scallops in a shucking box, take a knife, cut the muscle out into a bucket, and flick the shells overboard. We kept doing this 24/7 until the trip was over, usually in ten to seventeen days. We washed the scallops, put them in bags of forty to fifty pounds, then iced them in the fish hole. Then when we got to the dock, we would unload them, take five or six days off, and then do it again. This was extremely hard work!

A few years prior to this, a few of my friends would go to New Bedford, MA, to crew the scallop fleet. Today it is the biggest money-making port in the USA, and it is steeped in history. These guys used to go scalloping in the winter months because lobstering was only profitable in the summer and fall. This is one of the most dangerous jobs that you can do, but the money was good. A special friend of mine had gone out on a boat called The Navigator, and on the return trip, it went down. All those aboard perished. I remember it like it was yesterday. My friend's name was Ricky, and I loved him like a brother. There is a plaque at the whaling museum with the name of the crew. Every time I made a trip past Round Shoal Buoy, I would say a prayer for Ricky. Many a good man has gone down in boats trying to make a living on the sea.

My dad had a heart attack while I was out fishing, but again, after I found out he was okay, I just decided to stay with the boat and get high. I didn't like being on deck, and I wanted to be a captain. I felt I could do so much better than the other captains I had been working for, but my addiction was standing in my way. Things started to get really crazy on the boat, and I finally quit and headed back to Maine.

While I was away, the Feds had busted the head dealer from New Hampshire in the pot running operation that I had been involved in, and in turn, he gave us up. They ended up putting one of my friends, who had done all the planning, in prison for a five-year sentence. He did all our time for us. They stopped the investigation after that. As I said before, God saved me from many scrapes, and this was one of them!

34 | A Fall to Grace

Michael Swordfishing Pt. 1

Michael Swordfishing Pt. 2

Chapter Four: Fishing—A Way Of Life | 35

Chapter Five:
Commercial Scalloping – The Big Time

For the love of money is a root of all kinds of evil.
Some people, eager for money, have wandered from
the faith and pierced themselves with many griefs.

1 Timothy 6:10

I needed to make a quick buck, so I headed to Gloucester, MA, because I had heard there were a few Highline boats from New Bedford fishing out of there. They had pulled out of New Bedford because the mob had control of the fish buyers and were controlling the price of scallops. A few of the boats took the risk to leave New Bedford in protest. This was a whole different world than the one I had been fishing in. These boats and crews were professional, and if you didn't have the skills or the backbone for it, you might as well have gone home. I got to Gloucester, and there were a couple of boats there, the Westport and the Canton, which were sister ships. The Canton had an all-Maine crew, and the Westport had an all-Massachusetts crew. I got hired on the Westport as a transit (for one trip), and of course, I lied and told the captain that I was really experienced. There was a real rivalry between Maine and Massachusetts. I guess it was just a part of history, ever since Maine broke off from Massachusetts back in the 1800s.

We set out on our first trip with Captain Eddy, who was such a great guy. There were eleven people on the boat. We steamed to the northern edge of Georges Bank, about one hundred sixty miles offshore, and started fishing. I was a hook-up man, and I put the hook in the drag to bring it aboard, then used the hook to dump it out, and then put it back overboard. Tommy was my winch man and taught me the ropes. This is where I really grew up and learned what hard work and teamwork were all about. I just about killed myself to keep up, and after a six-hour watch, I just ate and crawled into my bunk. We had a little over 20,000 pounds of scallop meat that trip and the count of meat was fifty to sixty scallops per pound. These were small scallops, and by today's regulations, we wouldn't have fished on the stuff. We got to the dock and unloaded. We always settled at a local bar, and this time, we went to the Crow's Nest. I was a transit and was probably the worst scallop cutter on the boat, but I worked my tail off doing everything else. I was so beaten up that I could barely lift my beer up to drink from it! Captain Eddy walked in and started passing out the checks. He got to me and said, "You're not the fastest cutter, but you have a big heart, and you worked your tail off! I talked to the crew, and they decided you should get a full share. I'm offering you a full-time job. What do you say?" Well, of course, I said yes, and so I became a scalloper!

On our second trip, we did the same thing, 20,000 pounds in meat, and we were on a roll. When I got paid, I stopped in Rt 128 Cycles and bought a 500 cc Yamaha motorcycle, even though I didn't have a license! I wasn't worried; I just put the plates on it, and off I headed to Maine.

My mom and dad had sold the house in Florida and bought a house in Rockland, Maine. Now I had a place to crash after I ran out of money, which was every trip. I ended up making seven or eight trips on the Westport and decided to quit because I was beaten up and tired of it. Before I quit, both the Westport and Canton were in on the same day, so a bunch of us decided to buy tickets to Fort Lauderdale, FL, to party. There were six of us, and between us, we had close to $12,000. We spent every dime we had on drinking and cocaine, and when we landed in Boston, we had just enough money to pay for parking! This is why I decided to quit. I was just going nowhere!

I decided to go home and maybe try to get a job lobstering

with my friend, who had gotten out of prison for stabbing the guy
he thought burned his house down. He had a beautiful forty-two
feet wooden lobster boat and wanted to rig it up for scalloping
in the winter. He hired me to design the gear and drag. I started
living with him in a cottage on Patten Point. This was when I met
my future wife. She was working in a bar called the Trackside, or
Fightside, as we called it. We started dating, and she more or less
moved in with us in the cottage. When we got the boat rigged
for scalloping, we headed Downeast, or up the coast of Maine, in
hopes of finding scallops. We put in at Southwest Harbor, then
Jonesport, and finally ended up around Cross Island off Bucks
Harbor, Maine. We were towing the first day off Cross Island, and
the other deckhand came running up to the wheelhouse and asked
us to check something out. He had this two-inch square of what
looked like shoe leather, but it smelled like hash. We found out
that the winter before, a barge loaded with hash had been towed by
a tugboat into Little Machias Bay. It was supposed to unload it, but
the Coast Guard got wind of it, and as they were headed to bust
them, the crew started throwing it overboard. It was in aluminum
containers, and the story was that the Coast Guard didn't want it
washing up on the shore, so they put holes in the containers, and
they sunk. Whatever happened, there was a ton of hash all over
that area. People were picking it up by bushel baskets at low tide
and selling it. We called it sea-hash and started fishing on it. We
caught chunks in all different sizes, but one brick was about the
same as a size 11 shoe sole and weighed half a pound. After we
dried it out, we started selling it for $500 per pound. It had the
word "MAZARI" stamped on it, so we knew it was real.

We brought the boat home, and after a few days, another
friend and I took the boat back to Buck's Harbor with our girl-
friends and started to fish on the hash. We would send the girls
back home with the hash, and our other friend would sell it.
We did this one whole winter. We caught about sixty to seventy
pounds of hash and caught a bunch of scallops! It finally ended

Chapter Five: Commercial Scalloping —The Big Time | 39

when several other boats from home showed up, and the Coast Guard started making checks. It was fun while it lasted!

We were on our way home, and I decided to try big boat scalloping again. There were a few boats in Rockland, Maine, at the time. The Sea Trek had a local captain, and the crew was from the area, so I went down and got a job. This was a little different than fishing out of New Bedford or Gloucester. It was a much smaller operation. We were fishing mostly Downeast, which was closer to home. Also, we were able to smoke lots of weed if we did our job. This was awesome until we started doing coke and pills along with the pot. The captain hired a local drug dealer to supply the coke, and it got so bad that one trip, we only steamed a short time, and the captain decided we needed some more coke, so he turned the boat around! Another time, the cook brought a bunch of Valium. One of the crew and I started taking them, and I woke up three days later! I had no idea where I was, and from what the guys told me, I had been working the whole time! Again, I feel God had been watching over me, but unfortunately, it was more of the same thing. Now I was staying high on the boat too, no more "seahab." I got into an argument with the captain about the drug dealer being on the boat, and I quit.

During all this time of mostly being offshore, my relationship had gone sour, and people were telling me that my girlfriend had been sleeping around, and it had become sort of a joke among people. So, I threw her out of the little place that I was renting and was heartbroken because I really cared about her. I decided at that point that I was going to show everyone that I wasn't a joke, that I was going to be a captain of a big scallop boat...end of story! So, I started the process of becoming a captain, and I got a job at the Harvey Gamage. The boat was owned by a family out of Camden, Maine, and they had three boats in their fleet—the Pocahontas, the Harvey Gamage, and the Shelmac. These were all wooden, eastern rigs. Captain Carl had the Gamage, and he was a really nice guy with a huge drinking problem. The only reason he

40 | A Fall to Grace

kept this job was probably that his dad owned the boat. I've got to say that Carl taught me more about scalloping in eight months than I could have ever imagined!

This is how it worked. Carl would show up to the boat drunk, pass out on the steam out, and the mate would do double duty until Carl sobered up. Then we would start fishing, and we always got a trip. In the winter, Carl loved to go to Nantucket to layover because of the weather. We would sell a few bags of scallops and get drunk for a couple of days or until the cops would run us out of town! During one of those trips, Carl asked me to be his first mate, and that was my big break! The drawback was that babysitting Carl made the job challenging! I guess it was the Christmas trip in 1986 when I got my shot at running as boat captain.

We were waiting for Carl so we could sail, and it was snowing and getting dark. I was in the wheelhouse, looking down the dock for Carl, and I spotted him staggering down to the boat. When he got down to the boat, he yelled up, "Sunshine, I need to talk to you." I stepped out onto the dock, and he said, "I'm not going on this trip; you're ready to be captain. I'll see you in ten to twelve days!" Then he walked off. I remember how nervous I was telling the crew, but they were all good with it, and I picked my first mate, and off we went, snowstorm and all. I went to one of our good spots off Nantucket and set the drags out but broke one of the middle steel bars on the first tow. This wasn't a good sign, and you could see it in the eyes of the crew. I said a little prayer, showed the mate where I wanted him to go, and went down and welded the bar into place. We steamed about four hours farther east and set out. I was sick to my stomach hauling back that first tow, and wouldn't you know it: we caught six to seven bushels of scallops on each side with a bunch of fish. At that time, 5–6,000 pounds would have been a nice trip, and we ended up with almost 9,000 pounds of scallops and 7,000 pounds of fish! It had to be that prayer! I can't tell you how I felt while bringing the boat into New Bedford Harbor. The crew was happy, and I was blown away!

We got a great price, and the owner was at the dock and pulled me aside. He said, "Nice job, the boat is yours!"

The second trip was better. We got out on time, and everything went according to plan. We got to the dock at about 3 AM, and as I was getting off the boat at the fish house, this girl came running up and jumped into my arms. It was the girl I had broken up with and swore I would never go back to. Well, she said she loved me and wanted to marry me and have kids, and that was exactly what we did! I put a ring on her finger, and we moved to Mattapoisett, MA. We rented this cool little cabin on Crescent Beach and got married. I should have known that it wouldn't work because the night of our wedding, I left by myself in my white tux and headed into New Bedford and went to the National Club. This was a pretty rough bar, and I got into a fight! I nearly got ripped out of my tux and proceeded to get drunk until the wedding party found me at about 3 AM. They took me home, and that's how my first wedding night went! My wife and I started really getting into the drugs until she got pregnant. She slowed down and stopped, but I kept going. I took the Gamage for seven trips, and then I got a call from a boat owner from Portland, ME. He owned a fleet of newer steel boats and asked me if I would be interested in taking The Prowler. Of course, I said yes, so I quit the Gamage and moved to South Portland, ME. Most of the crew went with me, and it was awesome to fish out of a Maine port.

This was a dream job for me, being able to captain a boat out of Maine and have a place to live right up the dock. We were really doing well with the boat, and I got in from a trip just as our son was born. He was a healthy boy with blonde hair and blue eyes. My wife was in labor for a long time, and I was just blown away by what had just happened. Unfortunately, I found a way to ruin the day because I decided to go out and celebrate the birth of my son. It started out alright but soon turned into a shot-drinking, coke-snorting event, and eventually, I decided to drive home from the bar at about four in the afternoon. As I was driving the wrong way down a one-way street, there happened to be an undercover cop on the side of the street with his car door open, and I hit his door, ripped it off, and kept going. Soon, five cop cars boxed me in, and they arrested me for leaving the scene of an accident and DUI. Off to jail I went and had to call my wife, who was still in the hospital, to bail me out! As you can imagine, she was not very happy about this, and this is how our relationship would go.

We named our son William Michael Ball, and I thought this was what was going to save me, that I would finally grow up, but that didn't happen. I was doing well catch-wise with the boat, and the owner was talking about building a new bigger boat for me, but my dirty little secret was that I had started to dabble in the needle again, and now I dragged my wife into it also. I was super jealous, and going away for a couple of weeks at a time didn't help! Then, when I got home, we would get high the whole time. It was a vicious cycle.

I ran The Prowler for a couple of years and got a call from a boat owner out of Boston, and he offered me a bigger, nicer steel boat. He also could give us a better price because he owned a seafood company. He was Italian and, I think, "connected." So, I quit The Prowler, and off I went to Boston. The boat at the time was rigged for a different kind of fishing. The owners had me bring it to New Bedford and had it completely redone. I would go down and stay on the boat for three to four days a week and supervise the job. This gave me a chance to go out at night, and this is when I really started using heroin. Lots of crazy things were going on in New Bedford, and one time, I woke up on the boat early and decided to go to breakfast. As I got off the boat and walked down the dock, right behind our boat, I could see a car underwater, and it looked like there was a body in the back window. I ran to a nearby bait shop and told the guy to call 911. The cops got there and said it was just trash in the window, so I went to breakfast with the boat owners. As we were driving into the parking lot, there was a pile of cop cars and other law enforcement people milling

Chapter Five: Commercial Scalloping —The Big Time | 43

around. As they were hauling the car out of the water, there *was* a dead guy rolled up in the passenger side window, and once the cops saw me, they came over and started questioning me for a while. They said that the guy had committed suicide, but it really looked suspicious to me. The owners couldn't understand how I didn't hear the commotion, especially since I was on the boat. If they only knew!

As this new job unfolded, what I didn't realize was that I had an ego that was the size of Texas and an inferiority complex, if that makes any sense! What I believe today is that as soon as I smoked that first joint at twelve years old, my emotional growth really slowed down, and I was this little scared kid inside a man's body. I thought that I didn't fit into a very big world. Having a huge drug habit only made things worse.

We got the boat done in the late summer, but fishing as a whole was on the decline, and trips' catches were dropping off from over-fishing. Also, a few years earlier, the USA and Canada had drawn a line across Georges Bank, called The Hague Line, which took away prime scallop bottom that we used to be able to fish. Its effect had bunched all the USA boats into a small area, and we cleaned it out of scallops. As modern-day "pirates," we jumped the line into Canada, loading the boats up and then steaming back into the USA waters to cut the scallops out. I had done it with The Prowler, and I had started to do it with the new boat, The Nautilus. It was the same feeling as drug smuggling when you had a deck full of scallops, and you were steaming for the USA line, many times with the Canadian Coast Guard chasing you! At first, they would stop at the line, but after a while, the USA stepped in, and fishermen started getting busted. Eventually, the fisheries' authorities started putting these tracking devices on the USA boats, so there was no way of going over the line without them knowing about it.

We started fishing out of Boston with The Nautilus, so it was quite a steam to Georges Bank but closer to the Great South

44 | A Fall to Grace

Channel. We were using thirteen-foot drags, so they were bigger than the ones on The Prowler, and the boat was also ten feet longer than The Prowler. I think The Prowler was a better seaworthy boat, meaning it was more comfortable in rough weather. We were fishing on twelve-to-fourteen-day trips and trying to get out on the fifth day home.

The auction house we sold at was on the same pier that we kept the boat at, so it was convenient. The boat owner's cousin ran the auction, so as I said, it was all connected. The fish house was also owned by the same family, so they bought most of our scallops. The owner of a large chain restaurant was just getting started and used to call us on the way in and order anywhere from 2,000 to 6,000 pounds of the freshest scallops. Occasionally, the cops would show up at the boat, and the owners would come down and grab a couple of forty-pound bags of scallops and throw them in the trunk of the cruiser. Again, all connected.

At one point, a whole fleet of Vietnamese fishing boats docked at the pier and was going to fish out of Boston. There must have been fifteen to twenty boats tied up when we left for a trip. Five days later, when we got back, every one of the boats was on the bottom! Someone had sunk them all! We got the point: you don't mess with the family!

Another time the owners called me into the office and showed me some pictures of a guy supposedly selling drugs to some of my crew and asked me if I knew anything about it. I really didn't, so I told them I would keep an eye out for the guy. They said it had already been taken care of, and we never saw that guy again. I knew that I had to be very careful about my drug use, or I would be fired, no questions asked!

At one point, my mate was getting really cocky, and he knew about my drug use. He decided he would tell the owners about it and take the boat out from under me. Again, I got called into the office, and they questioned me about it. They assured me that they

Chapter Five: Commercial Scalloping —The Big Time | 45

trusted me, and they asked me to fire the mate, which I did right away! Many years later, he died from a drug overdose. Crazy how addiction works. It takes your soul; then it kills you! This saying has stuck with me for years: "No God, no peace; know God, know peace." Unbelievably true!

The wife and I decided to buy a house in Portland, Maine. We had a friend who was a real estate agent, and we found a beautiful four-bedroom, two-bath older colonial for sale. We went to the bank, and to my surprise, they approved the loan. It was in a great neighborhood with a nice, fenced backyard, and it had a small, detached garage for a shop. My dad and brother came over and built a big deck on the back.

My brother was living in South Portland, and he had gotten into fishing at some point. He had met a girl in a fisherman's bar called Angie's, and she was the bartender. Angie's was part of the Three Doors of Hell on Commercial Street on the waterfront of Portland. It was called this because there were three bars all in a row, and crazy things ended up happening there. When I ran The Prowler, we used to settle at Angie's. I would meet my wife and son there and wait for the checks. It was kind of like a big extended family.

My brother and this girl did all kinds of hiking and mountain climbing until one time, he fell off one of the mountains that they were climbing and broke his back and leg. This ended his fishing career, but she stayed with him, and they got married. He asked me to be his best man, so just after I had gotten in from a trip, the next day I went to his wedding. I had a pocket full of coke and was quite drunk before it started. The wedding was at this real swanky club in Cape Elizabeth. A bunch of her rich family and relatives came, and I was a real trainwreck. Somehow, I got through the ceremony, and eventually, someone found me passed out in the bushes outside the club. They stuffed me in a cab, and I woke up the next morning in a hotel room. I never got invited to another family outing with my brother again! He and I stayed in touch, and eventually, he went to college and graduated with an

46 | A Fall to Grace

engineering degree. He had a couple of kids and was living the life.

It seemed like my life was finally starting to come together, except for the fact that I didn't trust my wife, and we were doing lots of coke when I would get in from a trip. I couldn't stop working because we were just barely getting by with our drug habits, and this was causing a huge strain on our marriage. Even so, I really felt like I was growing up and becoming a responsible adult! I could run a boat anywhere in the world, people knew me and seemed to like me in the scalloping industry, I had a home, a wife, a beautiful son, and I was holding it together, sort of!

I ran The Nautilus for eighteen months, getting trips in, and it seemed the owners were happy. Then, after one of the trips, the owners wanted to have a talk with me, so they took me out to lunch. Needless to say, I expected the worst, but what happened next was unexpected! They offered to sell me the boat with all the permits, plus I could keep the boat at the fish house, and they would pay me fifty cents a pound over the New Bedford price. This was a dream deal! The total price was $750,000. Today that boat with the permits is worth a couple of million dollars, so it was a very good deal! All I had to do was mortgage our house, and they would co-sign the loan. It was pretty much a done deal. They thought I had a beautiful home life and that I was a great investment. But the truth was our marriage was on the rocks, and we were financially a wreck!

The very next trip, we were out on Georges Bank, and the port-side winch got stuck, and the bail of the drag was sticking upright and wouldn't go down. I went out on the deck to see if I could free it and as I was pushing on the bail, the brake let go, and the bail came crashing down. As it was coming down, I pushed myself off the bail, and as I did, the bail hit the main wire, and the wire shot out, hitting me in the forehead, flipping me up in the air, and I landed on the hatch cover. It knocked me out for a minute, and when I came to, I felt blood dripping down my face. I could tell I had a concussion, and I needed

Chapter Five: Commercial Scalloping —The Big Time | 47

stitches. If I only needed stitches, I would have taped the cut up, but the concussion worried me, so I cut the trip short and headed for the dock. I called the owners, and they understood and just wanted to make sure I was okay. I didn't realize how much this event would change my life and how many bad decisions I would make while dealing with this injury.

When we got the boat tied up and cleaned, I went to the hospital and got some stitches and a CAT scan, and they also checked my back, which was really hurting. They sent me home to take at least one trip off. I talked to my mate, and he would take the boat out on the next trip, so I headed home. The one bright spot in all this was I would get to spend some time with my son. I felt horrible and just wanted to relax, but that didn't last long. My wife was a little freaked out, to say the least, and we didn't have much money in our bank account. The tests came back, and I had a concussion but nothing conclusive about my back injury. The owners cut me a check, and I settled in to get well.

A couple of weeks went by, and my head had cleared up, but my back was still really sore, and my left foot was mostly numb, so I was getting a little anxious. It was nice spending time with Billy. He was growing so fast, and I had missed so much being offshore all the time. We were hanging out in the living room, and someone knocked on the front door, which was weird because everyone always came to the back door. I opened it, and to my surprise, it was a local lawyer asking me how I was. I later found out that lawyers aren't supposed to do this, but there he was. He asked if he could come in and talk. I figured I might as well listen to him, and he was smooth. He told me the owners of the boat would let the insurance company take advantage of me, and if I signed with him, we would all be fishing in a yacht down in the Caribbean for the rest of our lives. He said this case was worth millions if my back injury was what he thought it was. He was connected to a huge maritime injury law firm out of Boston that "never loses." He said they had their own doctors for me to see, and this was a "win-

win situation." My wife didn't like it, but I said I would think about it. With the lure of a big payday and feeling like the world owed it to me, even though the owners said they would stand by me through everything, I decided to go with the lawsuit! I signed the paperwork a week later. If only I had said a prayer and asked God what to do, I might have avoided this bad disaster!

The lawyer said they could keep a lid on this for a few months, but eventually, the insurance company would find out, and things would change. They just forgot to tell me how much! I had a bunch of tests done on my back and was told that I had a possible disc rupture. The owners told me to figure out my bills, and they would pay them. They started sending me a check bi-weekly, but because of our drug habits, we weren't making ends meet. We were fighting every day, and our son was in the middle of it. Thank God he was still very young, but I am sure he felt the tension. I got hooked up with this local drug dealer who was from Boston and became his bodyguard. At least that's what I thought because he would disappear, and his brother would call me from Boston and ask me to go find him and pull him out of the situation. I can't believe that I didn't get shot, as I was getting paid in coke! My wife was starting to leave with our son for a few days here and there because I was bringing these people into our house.

It all came crashing down in one big swipe. The owners got wind of the pending lawsuit. By law, they only had to pay me $25 per day under something called the Jones Act, and they were paying me significantly more, as well as paying my medical bills. They called me and were angry and hurt and told me that I had really screwed up!

The doctors had put this TENS unit on my back that would shock my back muscles to help with the pain. We had just installed a security system in our house because we were doing so much coke that we were getting paranoid. One night my wife and I got into a huge fight. She spat in my face, and I pushed her. She ran to the security panel and hit the panic button. The cops

Chapter Five: Commercial Scalloping —The Big Time | 49

showed up in a couple of minutes. She was crying and said that I had hit her and when the cops saw the TENS unit with red blinking light and wires coming from it, they handcuffed me to the telephone pole and called the bomb squad! Yep, there I was, handcuffed to a telephone pole, cops had their guns drawn on me, my wife was holding my son, who was crying, and she was calling me a wife-beater! The whole neighborhood was watching from their porches! The cops finally realized it wasn't a bomb, took me to jail, and charged me with domestic violence. The next day they let me out, but I couldn't go home. By then, my wife had cleaned out the bank account and left with our son.

I called one of my friends from the Midcoast area where I had been as a teenager, and he sent his wife down to get me. I stayed with them for about a month or so until I decided that I needed to head back closer to my home. I was going to rent a condo in Old Orchard Beach. I had worked with my friend for a little while and saved up a few bucks, plus I still had a check from the boat owners, so I rented this nice condo on the water. I called my lawyers, expecting them to start paying my way, and they told me that was not the agreement, to read the contract. They would give me rides to their doctors but would not pay my rent. I was to get $25 per day. They said to look at the bright side, the more I lost financially and the more drugs I became addicted to amounted to more money in this "huge" settlement. I believed them, and I got sucked in one more time.

I stayed in the condo for about three months, and my wife went to court to get sole custody of our son. Of course, she got it, and I would get to see him on occasion. The lawyers found a back surgeon who said I needed surgery on my lower back, and his opinion was that I probably would not ever be able to make a living on the ocean again. My lawyers were ecstatic! They could smell blood in the water. I got kicked out of the condo because my money was running out, so I got a small basement apartment in Old Orchard Beach. I was getting paid just enough to make rent, food, and medication. I finally had my surgery in Portsmouth, NH, and my lawyers set a trial date. The insurance company had offered us $35,000, but my lawyers said, "No way," so I turned it down.

One day I got a call from one of my neighbors in Portland saying she had been watching the house because my wife had gone somewhere with her new boyfriend. When the neighbor had gone to check on the house, she noticed that the furnace was off, and it was getting cold out. I had been told by the judge to stay away from the house, but I still couldn't let the pipes freeze, so I headed there, and sure enough, the furnace was broken. I called a furnace repairman, and as he was headed over, I figured I would just check out the house. To my surprise, there was no doubt that another guy was living there. I was angry and heartbroken at the same time. I got the furnace fixed and headed back to my apartment. When she got home, she knew I had been there, and she threatened to call the cops if I ever went there again.

I spent the winter freezing in this basement apartment, and finally, the day came for the start of this trial. The lawyers brought me to Boston, put me up in this really nice hotel, and prepped me on how to act. The owners of the boat had been insured by Lloyd's of London, and they had seven lawyers of their own. We started the jury trial, and things were going smoothly until I was put on the stand and asked if I had ever hurt my back before. I answered, "No." This is what I truly thought, but I realized that I had been on a boat before, and we had taken on a big wave, and I had tweaked my back. I finished the trip, and when I got in, I went to the emergency room, basically to get some painkillers. They never took an X-ray. I went right back out fishing afterward. In the deposition, I had said "No" also, so they got me for contempt of court. My lawyers said if I didn't drop the lawsuit, I would have to pay all the court costs. They said to just walk away, and I did.

I remember that bus ride back to Portland. I called my wife, and she was so mad she told me never to talk to her again. At that point, I decided I might as well kill myself. When I got off the

Chapter Five: Commercial Scalloping —The Big Time | 51

bus, I started walking over the South Portland bridge, and I was going to jump off it, but God intervened. He is amazing that way! My brother just happened to be driving across the bridge and saw me. He put me in his truck, took me to his house, and kept me there for a couple of days until he found a rehab that I could go to.

He found a drug rehab in Westbrook. It was a fourteen-day program, and they took me right away. This helped with the depression but giving up drugs was another issue. Everyone in there had some serious issues, including me! I started telling everyone that I was a boat captain and made a ton of money. My ego was working overtime! Sad when I think about not being able to get real, but even in rehab, I wanted to fit in, to be someone special, so I played the role. I started feeling better after a few days and started thinking about getting back to scalloping again. I was sweet on a couple of girls in there; you know, sick people love sick people! So, we planned to hook up when we got out. My wife did bring my son to visit, and that always really cheered me up. I just loved seeing him. Just before I got out, one of the guys pulled me aside and told me he had two ounces of coke in his car and wanted to know if I needed a ride to Old Orchard Beach. Of course, I said yes, and off I went on another coke binge!

After a few days of partying with the girls from rehab, I decided it was time to head to New Bedford and get a job. Off I went and landed an amazing job on one of the newest boats in the fleet! Also, we were taking her sister ships, The Endeavor and The Courageous. I started on deck, and they had three crews for two boats, and we would rotate boats. The boats were highliners of the fleet, meaning they were making big money. I was flying high, but I started using heroin when I was not working. I tried to get home to Maine every trip and give my wife some money for my son. Sometimes she would let me stay a couple of days, and we would almost be a family again, but it always ended, and I would go back fishing again. After a few months, I got the mate's job, and we were doing amazing and making big money, but again, I would

52 | A Fall to Grace

spend it all and be broke on the day we sailed.

The captain had given me several opportunities to straighten out, and he finally fired me for showing up high. I bounced right back and got another job on another good boat, which I kept for a few trips. This ended up being my life for the next few years, going from boat to boat until they figured me out, then I would quit. I finally ended up on a boat called The Chief with another great captain. I got the mate's job, and I turned my partying down a bit because we were fishing out of Groton, Connecticut. There was plenty of coke, but dope was hard to find, so things were looking up. The Chief was a little smaller boat than the others, but it was just a beautiful boat with a nice captain and owner. They also had a smaller boat that had caught my eye; maybe in the future, I would think about asking to run that boat as a captain. We would unload our scallops, ice up and fuel up the boat in Stonington, CT. That was a beautiful port. When we tied up in Groton, the next dock over on the river was Electric Boat Company, which built the Seawolf submarines. There were submarines always coming and going. This was such an awesome sight!

There were a few bars along the shore, and we used to drink at one of them often. There was a waitress who worked there whom I really liked, and her name was Brandy. It was like I was living in that song from the '70s. I ended up dating her a few times because her boyfriend had gone to prison. She had a small son. I fell in love with her at first sight, but after a few dates with me getting coked out of my mind, she moved on, so I started going home to Maine for a few days to be with my son, then I would head back to Groton a few days early to party and live on the boat. Then I would go fishing and sober up at "seahab" and do it all again.

On one trip, I was walking down to the boat quite hungover, and we always had to climb around these pilings on the dock, but this time there was ice on the wire holding them together, and I slipped and fell about eight feet down and landed straddling another wire. I felt my back go, so I crawled up the pile onto the

Chapter Five: Commercial Scalloping —The Big Time | 53

boat and went into the galley to lie down. The captain came down and asked what had happened, and he took me to a walk-in clinic. They told me they couldn't do any tests until the swelling went down, so I had to take the trip off. I went home, but I was pretty freaked out because of my last experience! I went to the local hospital in Maine, and they did an MRI and found another ruptured disc in my lower back. I found a surgeon at Maine Medical Center in Portland to do the surgery. This time the boat was paying for everything, so it was all good, except it took a while to get in for the surgery, and I was taking tons of painkillers. Now I had also found a steady connection for heroin.

Scalloping

Chapter Six:
The Gig Was Up

There is a way that appears to be right,
but in the end it leads to death.

Proverbs 14:12

I was renting a small apartment in Thomaston, Maine, at this point, and my mom was very sick. My dad had given up drinking and was taking care of her at home. I knew she didn't have much time left, so I went home to see her. I was high, and she saw how worried I was about her. She looked into my eyes and said everything was going to be okay. To this day, that still haunts me. I couldn't even stop taking drugs for one day to go see my mother. To be honest, I was always high, even when I had my son. What a waste of a human being!

A few days later, my dad showed up at my place early in the morning and told me Mom had passed. I felt numb. Dad had a funeral for her, and a bunch of her relatives and friends showed up. I was high and was passing out Valiums by the handful. To this day, there are people who haven't forgiven me for that. It was one of many things I wish I could take back or redo, but I can't.

The insurance company settled with me for this most recent injury and cut me a check for $20,000, which I used to buy a thirty-six-foot wooden Novi lobster boat. I had a few friends left who helped me out with some old lobster traps, and I started lobstering again out of South Thomaston. I was living in Thomaston (a different town), and the deal was that you were supposed to own land in the town you fished, or you would suffer the wrath. I found a guy to finance a piece of land in South Thomaston, and my dad co-signed a loan for a new single-wide trailer, and I was in business!

I had about 600 traps my first season and did okay. I was taking my dad and a friend as deckhands, so I didn't have to use my back all that much. I had decided to keep the boat in Owls Head because the owner of the dock had financed some lobster traps for me, so I sold my lobsters off his dock. The friend I was taking with me had a big prescription for painkillers, so he kept us jacked up all season. I had started dating this girl who had a couple of kids, and I had moved in with her for a while before I got the trailer.

It seemed like things were starting to work out. My son, Billy, was coming to visit more often, and my wife (still!) had seemed to sort of straighten out. The next season I had a full 800 traps. That's the limit that we could fish with a Maine lobster license. I had a decent spring catch-wise. My new girlfriend wanted me to get divorced, so I did, and I only had to pay the ex $1,000 because she showed up late for the hearing. She had gotten into some trouble, so I got custody of Billy, and he moved into the trailer with us. As the season went along, I kept doing better and had a few 1,000-pound days, so money was flowing like honey. But I was starting to get into the painkillers pretty heavy and some heroin occasionally. It didn't take long before the girlfriend had enough and left.

It was just my son and me. I was not very good at being a parent, so Billy used to stay at friends' houses or at my dad's (Gramps), especially when I was partying or chasing women. I used to get into fights with my dad all the time because I had him hold most of my money. This way, the trailer would get paid for, and Billy would have food and clothes. Billy was playing pee wee football, and I would show up at practice or games and throw all the kids into my truck and take them to Dairy Queen. I was trying to act like a great dad, but I was always high.

My ex-wife had gotten cleaned up again, and she knew what

58 | A Fall to Grace

I was doing, and she was really on my case, telling me Billy would be better off with her. I was still resentful about the past and wouldn't listen. Eventually, I was doing twenty to thirty bags of heroin a day. It was getting out of control, and I knew my son knew what I was doing, but he loved me too much to turn me in. Wow, writing this sure does hurt! What was I thinking, doing this to my son?

One afternoon I got a call from my dealer asking if I could go to New Bedford, MA, and pick up some dope. I was running out and starting to get sick, so I said yes, not thinking that my son had his championship football game that night. I knew my ex-wife was going to be there, too. At this point, I needed God terribly. My drug addiction became more important than my son! That's how bad addiction had me! I left with my dealer and headed to New Bedford. I have tried, but I will never totally get over the hurt this causes me every time I talk about it or look into my son's eyes, even today! The dealer gave me a few grand and let me out in New Bedford. She headed back to Maine, and I started looking up old friends to get dope.

What I didn't know was that the Feds had been watching my dealer for a couple of months. They knew that I had gone down with her, so I was on their radar. I got a room and bought a bunch of coke, but I had to wait for the dope for another day. I partied all night and didn't get any sleep. It ended up being another two days before the dope showed up. By then, I was so whacked out, and it hit me what I had done to my son. My ex had taken him back with her to Portland. I finally got the dope and got on a bus from New Bedford to Rockland, ME. The Feds thought I was coming back with my dealer, so they had my trailer staked out, but somehow, they lost me in New Bedford. I finally got in late and hadn't slept for days, so I crashed on my couch. I thought about killing myself, but I passed out instead, so I really believe that God was going to do for me what I couldn't do for myself. As I was passed out, I heard someone knocking on the door, so I came

Chapter Six: The Gig Was Up | 59

to and opened the door to cops, wardens, and guns! They busted me for a pile of dope. I just sat back down on the couch and felt numb. My dealer showed up at the house about thirty minutes later, and they busted her also. The Feds took her all over town doing "stings" and busting people.

Meanwhile, they took me to a holding cell in the local jail. Back then, you didn't get methadone or Suboxone to taper down. They put you in a paper suit and stuffed you in a cell to shake and bake.

While I was in jail on a probation hold pending new charges, I got my dad to get a good lawyer. He came in to see me and felt that I would probably just get a small jail sentence and lots of probation. The newspapers had printed the story and painted me as being a drug "kingpin" bringing all the heroin into Knox County, and with this bust, they had put a huge dent in the drugs flowing into Maine. The real dealer was never mentioned. The court had finally set bail, and my dad put my trailer up for collateral. I had to go to a halfway house for a year in Portland. *No problem*, I thought. I started going to tons of recovery meetings, and it looked like maybe they would cut me a break. But the monkey on my back had other ideas!

My roommate at this halfway house was a doctor who had lost his license, and he had a stash of Xanax. He said he would give me all I wanted if I would just go to the ER and get some painkillers. Part of my bail conditions was to remain clean (no pills), but my disease said, "Go ahead, what's the worst that can happen?" My life couldn't get any worse, so off to the hospital I went to, and I got the pain meds. After the deal, I started taking Xanax, got caught in a urine test, and was kicked out of the house. I took a bus back to Rockland, hit the local quick care for a few more pills, and went back to my trailer. The cops showed up a few hours later and threw me back in jail without bail.

I was back in a detox cell, which basically consists of a cell with a hole in the floor to vomit into. There was no mattress or

60 | A Fall to Grace

anything else so that a person couldn't hang themself. It was as cold as a refrigerator. I told them I wanted to kill myself, so I was on suicide watch. I had never felt lower in my life. My lawyer visited and told me that I really messed up and was now looking at maybe a year of prison time. I was guilty of getting the drugs, but I was just a junkie, *not* a kingpin drug dealer, and I was screaming for help but still holding onto my ego! How sad is that?

The DEA talked to me, and I told them that the only way to stop the flow of dope into Maine was to stop and search every car at the toll booth. Taking me off the street only meant there were three more who would start selling right behind me. When people had money to spend, the drugs were sure to be close by. I was just a fisherman who had a family history of addiction and needed help. They responded that if that was all that I could give them for information, then they were going to go after the full extent of the law to sentence me because of the amount that I had. That is exactly what they did!

I ended up getting eight years for trafficking, eight years for conspiracy, and one year for probation revocation. That was seventeen years for a drug addict! They did drop it to eight years with all but forty-two months suspended and four years of probation. In today's system, a person would get a year or even probation only. As they transported me to the prison in Windham, ME, I had some time to reflect on what I had done. I would only be able to see my son if my dad brought him. I told my dad to sell my boat and traps to pay for my mortgage. I also asked him to rent my trailer out while I was gone. I had failed in life, once again, due to my addiction and poor decisions.

When I got to prison, they took me through intake and strip-searched me. Then I got prison-issue clothes, which were bright orange. Then they put me in the pods with one other inmate. Here I was locked up for twenty hours a day until I was classified as minimum, medium, or maximum. I was hoping for minimum, which gives you a little freedom, and you can eventually get a job

Chapter Six: The Gig Was Up | 61

or maybe pre-release. When you get to the pods, everyone asks you what you are in for, and they want to see your paperwork to prove you aren't a child molester. Most, if not all, child molesters go into protective custody and are kept separate from the general population. I got classified as minimum, and I was so grateful. However, minimum was full, so I was sent up behind the wall in medium. Unfortunately, there was a guy who had been involved with me in a previous drug bust, and some of his friends thought that I had turned him in, and his friends were in medium classification. I remember walking up through the yard, scared, just praying so hard and hoping that I wouldn't get beaten. I had my dad bring the statement that his guy had written that proved that I didn't "rat" on him, and when I got confronted by a couple of his friends, I showed it to them. Thank God! It saved me! I was behind the wall for about two weeks and then was sent to the regular minimum section, which was overcrowded. We had four men in a cell and no room to put anything, but we got to use the gym, and we had a big yard to walk in. I got in a couple of fights with younger guys and won both, so no one messed with me. I had a couple of people I hung with, but mostly, I was by myself. From Windham, if you were minimum, you were sent to one of three work camps: The Farm in Cushing, Charleston–which was in the middle of nowhere—or Bucks Harbor in Downeast, Maine. I wanted to go to The Farm, but they sent me to Charleston, which was basically a logging camp!

Before I left Windham, I got to do some outside work, and one of our jobs was to clean out an old probation office in Portland. We went in, and while packing things up, we found some confiscated drugs and hard liquor! Can you imagine what a bunch of inmates would do with access to this stuff? We found a whole card of Valium and split it between us. I took five Valium on the way back to prison. They strip-searched us and let us back in. I woke up the next morning in my bunk, covered in chocolate cake, and had no idea what had happened. I guess a bunch of us blacked out and never got caught.

62 | A Fall to Grace

You could buy anything you wanted if you had the money. A lot of guys were making $1,000 per week selling cigarettes. The guards would bring them in and get a cut of the profit.

I finally got word that I was being shipped to Charleston, so I packed up what I had, and off we went. It was a three-hour drive north. Charleston was an old Air Force installation that had no fences and a bunch of barracks. It was winter, so we cut wood and brought it back to either burn in the wood furnaces or cut into lumber to build furniture and other wooden things to sell. When we got there, the snow was about three feet deep, and it was about minus twenty degrees! They took us to a shed and told us to strip down, bend, and cough, then they gave us new clothes, and we were sent to our new homes!

Because Charleston was a logging camp, there was an industrial arts program where you could earn money making things with wood. I started out in the wood kiln department. We would take the wood boards that were cut in our sawmill and dry them in these big kilns. It was a lot of work, but we got paid 50 cents per hour, so, at the end of the week, I had a few bucks to spend at the commissary. They also had Alcoholics Anonymous meetings, and I started attending them once a week.

You could still get drugs there if you had money or something to trade, so I was getting a few painkillers every other week. I had been there about a month and had paid for a couple of Darvocet. It's a large pill, so I crushed it and snorted it. The guards informed us they were doing a urine test on the whole dorm. If I got caught, I would be sent back to Windham and get extra time tacked onto my sentence. I was praying because I knew I would test positive, and I didn't want to screw up this opportunity to stay there. As they were lining us up to be tested, they stopped two people in front of me and said that was it, no more testing! For some reason, this feeling came over me that I can't explain other than it was the Holy Spirit telling me that the "gig" was up; it was time to start a new life. There was a new program for addicts starting in Wind-

Chapter Six: The Gig Was Up | 63

ham that I heard about, and the next day I wrote a letter asking the director to accept me into this new program. A week later, I was on a bus back to Windham!

This program was separate from the prison but still onsite, and it was for all types of addicts, run by the inmates and facilitated by professional staff. Like a boot camp for inmates, we had a special dress code and strict rules to follow. The program was eighteen months long, and after a person achieved all five levels in Windham, they graduated and got to go to pre-release in Hallowell, ME. Quite a few people washed out of the program while I was there. Each level demanded a little more responsibility, but we also got to give feedback or offer an opinion on the program. We were kept separated from the others in an old wing of the prison, which we cleaned and painted. There were two people in a cell, and we were locked down seven hours per night.

We did our own laundry. When someone was out of line, we did "stern concerns," which required the person who was out of line to stand facing the other person. The first person would yell at you and tell you how you messed up, and you couldn't say a word or react. The next person would tell you what you could have done better, and the third person would tell you about your good qualities and give you some positive feedback. I reacted a few times, which required a consequence, such as wearing a sign saying, "I am a reactor" or "I am not the captain of this ship." I had to do this until I admitted what I did and made amends for it. It was really hard for me! I had to be broken and built back up a bunch of times. I feel that it was a great program, and it helped many people get over themselves.

It was great to see my son more often by being in Windham, but it was terribly emotional for me when he left. It always made me feel very sad but determined to make it through the program. God placed a few good people in my path, for which I am grateful. One guy was Howard. He had been a sniper in the Marine Corps and was quite crazy. He took me to my first Bible study,

64 | A Fall to Grace

which was run by two older women. What struck me most about these women was they had nothing to gain except trying to help us. That made an impression on me, and I decided to come back after I got out and help in the same way. I made it through my prison time with people like Howard and a few others who would call me out on my attitudes and mistakes and then help me get through it. My life started to have a focus, and God was all around me. Never in my wildest dreams did I ever believe this would be my direction. I remember looking out my window at the razor wire and wondering what was going to happen to me when I got out. I started really getting into Alcoholics Anonymous. We got to go to two to three meetings a week. I feel God got me to AA, and AA got me closer to God.

Howard and I achieved all the levels of the program together, and toward the end, we were pretty much running it. It was hard not to have some fun with the consequences that we passed down! When we talked to most of the guys in our program one-on-one, they would drop their guard and tell us some horror stories of their childhoods. So, you could really understand where they were coming from. It was just crazy what most of them had gone through. Both Howard and I graduated at the same time, and they had a big party with a great meal and cake. I finally understood that God had stepped in on my hurricane of a life, and the only way I was going to stop my destruction was to take away my freedom, and He did just that. What a blessing!

We both got on the bus and headed to pre-release in Hallowell, Maine. We were so excited about this because it meant after four weeks, we got to go to outside AA meetings. We also got furloughs to go home for a weekend. Things were looking up for sure! When we got to Hallowell, it was a group of old closed government buildings that sat high on a hill. It housed both the general population and our program, so we ate together, but we kept to one end, so we had a little space. By the time inmates were brought there, they just wanted to work and save some money before being released. There wasn't a lot of trouble. We had to serve a month onsite before we could work on the outside or go to outside meetings. While we waited, we focused on meetings that were brought into the building.

I met another guy named Richard, who became a friend. He was a very quiet dude, but I got to know him while running with him on an outside track. He had been in prison for twenty years for murder. He had caught his wife having an affair and punched the guy, who fell and hit his head and died, so Richard got twenty years for manslaughter. He had repented for his actions and just wanted to be left alone. He taught me how to run and how to let go of things that really bothered me. He also taught me how to be calm, which is not how I have been most of my life. I considered both Richard and Howard to be real friends.

I was approved for my first-weekend furlough and had been in prison for almost two years, so I had become what's called "institutionalized." It's a big word, but it means when your whole world has been changed for you, your time is not yours anymore, someone tells you what to do and when to do it, and you have no say in it. My dad picked me up, and the guards gave me a hard time because they hated the program I was in, but I got to leave. I was supposed to go straight to my dad's house, but I asked him to stop at a store so I could buy a scratch ticket. I was totally blown away by how nice the girl was who worked there. She called me "dear" and told me to have a nice day. Not many of those are in prison! My ex brought my son up, and we had an awesome few days together! Three friends stopped by, and the one who had done some prison time gave me $200! I gave him a huge hug! I wasn't supposed to see anyone, but I did anyway. It was a life-renewing time for me. I was so grateful for this temporary freedom, and I went back more determined than ever to start a new path.

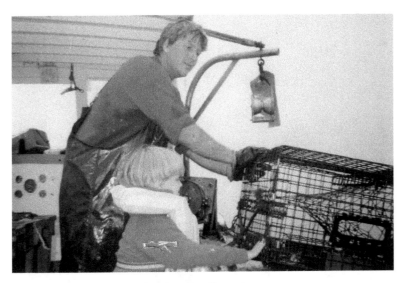

Michael and Billy Lobstering

Red Dragon Owls Head ME

Chapter Six: The Gig Was Up

Chapter Seven: Starting Over

Have mercy on me, O God, according to your unfailing love;
according to your great compassion blot out my transgressions.
Wash away all my iniquity and cleanse me from my sin.

Psalm 51:1–2

At this point, I had been clean and sober for over a year and was feeling healthy. I was running three miles a day and lifting weights. I put in for an outside work crew and got accepted to go clean and straighten headstones at the Veterans Cemetery. I also got to move furniture around some of the state buildings in Augusta. It was so cool to get out every day, no matter how hard I had to work! I also started to attend outside AA meetings, and I got to go to church. My faith was starting to come around, and everything seemed like a blessing. After my "trial period," I got to work at a real job doing some roofing for a former inmate who had started a company. We were working down around Searsport, ME, roofing some condominiums. I'm not much of a carpenter, but I got by. My dad bought me a tool belt with a nice hammer, and I remember how excited I was to get it. I put it on and wore it around like it was Christmas! I worked for the next six months, freezing my butt off, pounding my thumb, but grateful for every blister!

Speaking of Christmas, I used to sign up for this program called Angel Tree. This group would buy inmates' children's presents and hand them out over the holidays. My ex would take my son to church to attend a party and receive a Christmas present from "me." I will be forever indebted for this Christian program! In fact, my current wife supports this group financially as well as volunteers for them.

After a while, the prison took us to an AA meeting in Camden, ME. When I walked into the room, there was a tall, beautiful redhead speaking to some people I knew. I was totally caught off guard by how she made me feel, and I remember saying to myself, "That's the one." Little did I know. But again, God was doing for me what I could not do for myself. It was a powerful meeting because a bunch of my friends from the island I had growing up had gotten sober, and I got to connect with them; plus, I got to talk to that girl, and her name was Lori. When we left, I couldn't get her out of my mind.

Back at pre-release, I was going through the motions and was getting close to my release date. My friend, Howard, had gotten out a week before and was doing well, but I was really nervous about my release. I had found out about a program called "home confinement," and you could get out thirty days before your release date, so I signed up and was approved. I would be under supervision at my dad's house but felt that would be better than staying in pre-release. Finally, the day came; it was March 20th, 2003. It had been forty-one months that I had spent in prison. I still feel the sentence was excessive, and I wasted the first couple of years doing stupid things and hanging around toxic people, but now it was over! Dad came to pick me up, and as I was leaving, one of the guards who had been a real jerk said, "You'll be back," and he laughed. It took a lot to turn and walk away, but I did, and off we went. I was so overwhelmed with emotion that I cried most of the way home. The next morning, I went out for a run, and don't you know it, my probation officer had called, and I didn't answer. When I got back from my run, he was standing on the porch. He almost wrote me up on the spot and could have sent me back. He did a urine test and read me the Riot Act. Basically, I wasn't supposed to do anything unless he approved it.

I needed a job, and it just so happened that I had a good friend who lived across the street from my dad. His name was Dave, and we had fished together years before. He had cleaned his

70 | A Fall to Grace

act up, had a beautiful family, a really nice house, and a lawn care business. He was also on fire for God and recovery. I snuck across the street to have a talk with him. When I knocked on his door, I saw he was in this big hammock with his feet up right next to his wood stove. He had such peace in his eyes that I knew it was another God-direction, so I did two things. I asked him to be my sponsor, and then I asked him for a job. He said yes to both.

After the thirty-day home confinement, I was able to go to work and move around more freely. I would meet Dave around 7 AM and have coffee, and then we would head out to start a cleanup job. It was spring, and we weren't mowing lawns yet. We just raked and cleaned up properties, and once we would get it done, I would hit a meeting in hopes of seeing Lori. We did end up at a few meetings together, and I found out she was renting an apartment right around the corner from my dad's house! Now I had to ask her out. My son had come up to visit, and a bunch of my friends in the program and I were giving him a ride back to his mom's house in Portland. We were going to hit a meeting down there also. After we dropped my son off, we went to a meeting, and after the meeting, I asked Lori if I could talk to her. I finally got brave enough to ask her to have coffee, and she said yes! That started our courtship. On the second date, I asked her to come to church, and she cried through the whole mass. That's when I knew we were meant for each other!

Things were simple and good. My dad had kept my trailer rented while I was away, so he told the tenant that as soon as the lease was up, I was moving back. One day, my sponsor, Dave, took me to the local Chevy dealership for what I thought was a clean-up job. When we got there, he said to pick out a used car, and he would co-sign a loan for me. I was so humbled by this act of kindness that I had to turn away and wipe the tears away. I bought a Malibu, and I was so proud to drive it to Lori's place that night!

The lawn care business was not really my cup of tea, so I started looking for another opportunity just as a friend bought

Chapter Seven: Starting Over | 71

this forty-foot scallop boat, which was moored down in Chatham, MA. I went over to talk to him, and he hired me to run the boat on the spot. I still had to get permission from my probation officer. He was okay with it; I just had to let him know when I came and went. Chatham was this beautiful coastal town on Cape Cod that had a small harbor and was close to the Great South Channel, which was a prime spot for scalloping. I packed my seabag and headed down with a crew of two. When we got there, the boat was in good shape, so we put fuel, ice, and food aboard and checked the drag. The next morning, we headed out. It was about a four-hour steam to the fishing bottom. It was nice because you had to go around Monomoy Island, which was always covered with thousands of seals. You could hardly see the beach. Then you went out through the pass to the edge of the channel, and that's where we would set out. We would deck load the scallops until we had around 600 pounds in scallop meat, then cut the scallops while we were steaming in. There were about five to six pounds of meat per bushel of scallops. That is how we would work around the 600-pound limit. We had to have the scallops cut out before reaching the dock, so we would drop the drag overboard just outside the harbor and "cut out." Then we would go in and put the forty-to-fifty-pound scallop bags in a tote, ice them down, and get ready for the next day. We would fish for seven to eight days, then head home for a few days.

After the first trip, I was in the galley cleaning up the boat and spotted a pill bottle on the table. I looked at it, and it said "Vicodin," one of my favorite pills. I said a prayer, dumped it over the side, and confronted the deckhand who owned it. I fired the crew after that trip and told the owner that I wanted to hire my own people. I hired my sponsor, Dave, and another Dave, who I knew was a crackerjack scallop cutter, and we went on with our business. I had taken the boat for a few months, and both guys were getting ready to quit because living on a small boat really stunk. I was also really having a hard time being away from the love of my life, so we all quit and headed home.

I ultimately wanted to go lobstering, so I started looking for a small boat. I found a sixteen-foot outboard in Owls Head that a friend of mine had used, and he would sell it for $600. That night I was at Lori's place telling her about the boat, and out of the blue, she said she would lend me the money! I was again humbled by her selflessness and told her that I would pay her back. We had been spending a lot of time together, and one afternoon, she said that she wanted a commitment that we would be getting engaged and have no sex for a year! I agreed, which was a total Holy Spirit move because if you knew me, that is not how I used to roll!

Many of my fishermen friends had given me traps, rope, and buoys, so I jumped back into lobstering. It was so awesome to be back on the water, fishing on an outboard; it brought me back to when I was a kid—just free. I had two hundred traps and started doing well when shedders hit. Because I had a small boat, I could start hauling right at my mooring. I started catching a few lobsters; in fact, I had to come in and unload twice one day because I could only hold two hundred pounds in my boat safely. I had 420 pounds that day. All was good until I heard through the grapevine that a few people were saying that I was probably hauling other people's gear because they weren't doing that great. That just crushed me and made me more determined to buy a bigger boat and go harder! As far as lobstering goes, this time around, I owned property in the territory that I was fishing, so by rights, I was good.

The renters had finally moved out of my trailer, so Lori and I moved in. I took her to my mom's gravesite one day, and as we were praying, I got on one knee and asked for her hand in marriage. She said yes! Thank You, Jesus! We were so happy; there was no pressure or stress, just peace.

Billy came up from his mother's for the summer and spent a bunch of time with us, and he was really growing up. My ex-wife was doing much better by then, also. She had gone to college, had a good job, and provided a stable home for Billy. He was doing great in school and running track and became a top runner in his class.

Chapter Seven: Starting Over | 73

In those years, the lobsters would travel into very shallow water in the spring, and as the sun would heat up the water in early summer, the lobsters would dig into the mud for about two to three weeks. They would shed their old shells and grow new ones. Then they would start their journey back to deeper, cooler waters. We would start catching the "shedders" as they migrated around July 4th and have spurts of good fishing right through the middle of October. Then we would move the traps offshore and chase them until Christmas. Then most of us would take our traps up for the winter.

It was getting to that time of year when my little boat was too small to keep going, so I had to figure out what to do next. A good friend's dad was fishing off an island twenty miles offshore called Criehaven. He had his daughter working with him but needed an extra hand, so I took the job. His name was John, and I had known him since I was a kid. My dad even fished with him for a while. He had a beautiful home out on this island, so we would go out on two-to-three-day trips. This island was so peaceful. On the backside were cliffs, and I used to go there to pray and listen to the waves crashing below. It was just a magical place. This man took me under his wing, and he taught me so much about myself in such a short time. There were only about ten other fishermen who fished off this island, and I would go visit them and get the skinny on what was going on. John was a very private person and kept to himself, so I would come back at dinner and give him all the news. We would laugh and have a great time! He started giving me traps, buoys, and lots of rope for my next year. I got to take his boat a few times to haul his traps when he was away. When the deep of winter would roll around, he would stop by my place; we would talk and then go out for breakfast. I felt he was a second father to me.

Spring rolled around, and I got done fishing with John. Lori and I bought a thirty-four-foot Novi lobster boat and named it the Lori Lee. I was so excited to get going that I set out way too early, but I didn't care. Then one day, I was going to my truck at

74 | A Fall to Grace

Maine Coast, and one of my fellow fishermen stopped by and informed me that I shouldn't be hanging around the guys at that dock. There had been talk that if I wanted to fish offshore, I needed to tow their line. Well, I told this person I would do exactly what I wanted, and neither he nor any of those other guys were going to stop me! This was all because of an old dope deal and other dumb things that happened when we were younger, and it was still going on between a few fishermen. True to form, a few days later, I went out, and someone had cut off forty of my new traps! That means they cut the buoys off, and I lost the traps. This was done by people I knew and in the middle of my fishing area, where I had started fishing thirty years before. How sad is that? I still don't know who was responsible for sure, but if it weren't for God, I would have become unhinged, and that wouldn't have been good. I took it on the chin and moved on.

By the end of the school year, Billy came to live with us. I decided to give him the outboard and one hundred fifty traps so he could go lobstering, and he was stoked. Lori and I had decided on a wedding date, which was July 17th, 2004. She was like a little girl; it was really cool to watch. I had asked one of my good friends to be my best man and had all my ushers set. As we were getting our invitations out, the guy who had stopped by to tell me I shouldn't hang out with certain people came by and said he and his brother wouldn't be attending my wedding because they disliked my best man. Now, I had lived with both these brothers when I was younger and considered them good friends. When we were young, we were very tight, all of us. This kind of threw me for a loop, but he said it wasn't about me. Well, yes, it was about my wife and me! It was a real jerk move, one I've tried to put behind me for years, but there it is; I still get worked up about it! Small-town politics!

I set my son's gear, and all my traps were in the water. That's when Lori decided she wanted to work with me, so I started taking her as my sternman, as we called them. She was a real trooper because I was pushing to have a good year, and we had

Chapter Seven: Starting Over | 75

some good catches. The problem was I am very hard to work for, and if you weren't doing it my way, I would tell you. That works okay, except when it's your future wife, who has never been fishing and would cry at the drop of a hat. I spent time sitting on the hatch, hugging her, and telling her that I was sorry for yelling at her and that I would try to be better. That would usually happen at least once a week!

The wedding day rolled around, and we had invited about one hundred fifty people, mostly fishermen and our families. This was a sober wedding, so we were a little freaked out, to say the least! We got married in the Catholic church in Rockland, Maine. The priest was a guy who had been in my same class in school, and I had gotten him in trouble a few times! We did classes on having our previous marriages annulled per the Catholic religion, and we were ready. Lori has a big family, and they all flew in. It was so cool to do it right that time. The wedding went awesome! Lori looked like a princess! We rented a limo for the wedding party to ride together to the reception. When we got there, it was packed with sober fishermen, tons of friends, and of course, our families. I just couldn't believe it; another humbling moment. Everything was perfect, and we all had a great time. My best man, Jim, has long white hair and he always wears a bandana. He made the toast with sparkling cider, and it was very touching.

We had our honeymoon in John's house on Criehaven Island. We took the limo from the reception and headed to the lobster boat. As we came around the corner where the dock was, we saw the boat had been decorated with a ton of balloons and streamers. It was awesome! I rowed my wife out to the boat, and we headed offshore to the island, with balloons flying behind us. We spent two days on the island, walking the trails, sitting by the water, and just spending time with each other, with nothing else on our plates. It was perfect.

Her family was still in the area when we got back and wanted to go to haul (lobstering). I told them to be up early, dress accord-

76 | A Fall to Grace

ingly, and we would go. It was the middle of July in Maine, and we had a lot of fog that summer, so of course, that morning, it was thick as pea soup! To top it off, the family showed up in white shorts and tennis shoes! I took one look and thought, *OMG*, but I loved them, and they wanted to go, especially her dad, Enoch. He was a farmer who loved fishing and loved the Lord. I had about eight people on the boat, so it was quite cramped, and every time I would haul a trap up, they would all run to the side and see what was in it! I was hauling my shoal water traps close to shore in the eelgrass, so lots of mud was coming over the side and splashing everywhere. When they got off the boat, they were pretty much covered in mud, which had a distinct smell to it! I finally made the decision to drop them off on Tommy's Island, where my best man, Jim, had a nice house. This way, he could tell them some sea stories while I hauled some of my traps. I am sure they will never forget that day, for many reasons. We all had a great time, especially Lori's dad! He was just such a cool guy!

Billy was having a lot of fun hauling his own traps, and on occasion, I would take him with us. I am sure it was a little different living with us as a family. We would say grace before every meal, and we would go to church every Sunday. We didn't pressure Billy regarding our beliefs. He had made some new friends and had a whole gang of old friends from when he lived with me before. He had taken driver's education classes, so he had hopes for a car in the future. Fall was coming again, along with the windy weather, so we took up his traps, and hopefully, he would focus on school.

Lori and I made a good working pair, but she hated the windy weather, and she was prone to seasickness, so I knew our time together on the boat wasn't going to last. We made it another year with a few bucks in the bank, and we had our family together; what a blessing!

When I got out of prison, my hope, prayers, and dreams were: 1) to repair my relationship with God and my son, both devastated by my addiction, 2) to find a good Christian woman who I

Chapter Seven: Starting Over | 77

could partner with for life, and 3) to find a job to support my wife and son. That was it. The problem with dreams is that I always wanted more, and of course, even though I was clean and sober, my addiction was still very healthy.

We had decided to try to have kids right away, so Lori got pregnant that fall, and our lives seemed like they were going to change. Lori and Billy got along great, but Billy was starting to stretch us, and one day, Lori came to me after cleaning Billy's room and said she found a baggie with some pot in it. She was really freaked out, and I was a little upset, so we had the big talk with him, and I could see so much of myself in him. He had all the answers, but we could see a decline in grades, and he was always gone with friends. We grounded him, which just made him mad, but we moved on. As winter rolled on, Lori had a miscarriage, and it just devastated her. I'm so glad that we had God and each other to get through it. We did so much praying around it and decided to keep trying to have another child. Spring came, and we set our traps, but because of the long winter, we were broke and living off our credit cards. We were just surviving, and Lori got pregnant again. She started getting sick on the boat and finally quit to take care of herself. I hired a friend to go sternman; plus, I would take Billy on the weekends. Instead of being happy with what we had, I was already thinking bigger boat, all new traps; that is what I needed...*more*! We were having a good year financially, so I started looking for a bigger boat and found a beautiful forty-two-foot Duffy down in Harpswell. I made an offer on it, and the guy accepted! There was a lot of pressure on my wife because she would have to get the loan because I didn't have much credit. She also had another miscarriage and was mentally wrecked over it. Instead of slowing down, I, being the good addict that I was, just told her it would all be okay; I'd make more money with this new boat. So, she signed the papers, and I brought the boat home. Looking back, I was so selfish. The only reason I got a big boat was to show those so-called friends that I wasn't a failure. I got to haul a few times that fall with the new boat, called the "Lori Lee." Our second haul was 1,000 pounds, so I was feeding my ego.

We had a good year, and as I was taking my traps up, Lori found a lump in her breast. We went in and had a bunch of tests done, and it turned out to be cancer. I remember sitting with her, waiting for the doctor, scared, not knowing. Then the doctor came in and told us it was cancer and what our options were. We both cried and then hugged and set out to beat this thing. We did lots of praying! They did the surgery, and Lori decided to only do radiation, not chemotherapy. She had surgery in Portland, and the cancer didn't reach her lymph nodes. Thank God for that! They had inserted a balloon into her breast for the radiation, and as we were leaving Portland, she said, "Something just popped in my breast." So back to the hospital we went, and the balloon had burst! They tried again, but it wouldn't hold, so she had to do the regular radiation, which was five days a week for two months. We had to drive an hour each way. I drove her for the first month; then, because we were getting low on money, I decided to go to New Bedford and get a job scalloping. Lori was doing better, and a few of my good friends said they would give her rides; plus, I knew that a couple of bucks in the bank account would help her relax. So off I went. It's well known that I have no patience, and wouldn't you know it, God pointed me toward a boat named The Patience. The captain, whose name was Tom, was a Christian. Not only was all that awesome, but after I was hired as the first mate, Tom asked me if I knew someone who would cook on the boat. The night before, my friend and sponsor, Dave, had called me asking that I find a job for him. So, I headed home to spend a little time with Lori and get packed to go.

New Bedford had been a place where I had made so many poor decisions. I had almost died from overdoses at least five or six times, so God had placed Dave with me to watch over me. God also found a job with a Christian captain to keep me straight. One of the cool things I got to do with Dave during my time in New

Chapter Seven: Starting Over | 79

Bedford was to look up some of the captains I had harmed and make amends to them. There were a few that I couldn't find, but the ones I did find were surprised and wished me well. It was surreal fishing out of New Bedford again because everything was still there, the bars and the places I used to stay. I kind of got a weird feeling in my gut that I didn't like, plus the fact that Lori was still not out of the woods yet.

There were other things on our plates; one was my dad starting to get frail. When I was home, he would call in the middle of the night because he had fallen out of bed and couldn't get up. We talked to him about assisted living, but that was a resounding *no*! We needed to be available to help him. Also, this was Billy's last year of high school, which was a big deal, and even though I wanted him to become a lobsterman, I knew in my heart that he needed to go to college. Lori was adamant about him going to college, also. Lori was close to being done with her treatments, and I was almost done with my springtime scalloping before setting out my lobster traps.

A week before Billy was to graduate, my dad got really bad, had a stroke, and basically never woke up. The doctors told me that he was not going to regain consciousness, so I needed to make the decision to unplug him from life support. My brother didn't want any part of it, so I made the decision to unplug him. It still freaks me out. I did get a priest to give him the last rites, and I must say that when my mom was dying, she was at peace because she knew God, but my dad fought until the last breath because of his lack of faith.

We laid my dad to rest beside my mom, and he had a military send-off. A bunch of his friends showed up. This time I was sober; thank You, Jesus. Billy graduated, and Lori ended her treatments—she was cancer free! I finished one more scallop trip and started to get ready for another year of lobstering. In addition to all this, we had to clean and sell my dad's house because he had a reverse mortgage on it, and the bank was going to foreclose, so we

80 | A Fall to Grace

put it on the market. We sold the house for a small profit and split it with my brother. It still seems weird to drive by the old place.

Lori started working at a local bank, and I was setting my traps along with helping Billy to set his. I also had been volunteering at a local food bank when I could, plus getting to a bunch of AA meetings. Billy had been accepted to the University of Maine at Orono, which was a couple of hours north of us. We all got through the summer and started getting Billy packed up for his freshmen year. He was going to stay on campus in the dorms that year. We got him the best deal we could. Lori had taken out a loan for his tuition, and Billy had also taken out a student loan. So, we were getting it done. We drove Billy up to Orono at the end of August, but he had only packed a few things and didn't look very excited. The dorms were full of students, and I was so proud because I wished I could have done this instead of quitting high school. He ended up coming home a few weeks later, packed up most of his things, and stayed up in Orono the rest of the year! I guess he found out it was going to be fun!

Lori and I decided to take a vacation that winter, so we picked the Dominican Republic, but I had issues with getting a passport, so we ended up going to Oahu and Maui. Lori had also bought Patriots tickets for Billy and me for our birthdays. We were both huge fans and had an awesome time down in Foxborough watching the Patriots beat the Dolphins! Our lobster season had ended, and we had a really good year, so I was feeling really moved to help people, also. I started going to the soup kitchen as much as I could. It would break my heart to see these single moms come in for a meal with their children. At the end of each meal, we had a few tables full of food for people to take home, and I would always put a few pies and cakes away for the kids. I just loved seeing their faces when I gave them a big cake!

I was hitting a bunch of AA meetings and sponsoring a few young men, plus I was going back to pre-release as much as I could. This was so therapeutic for me, especially going into prison to talk

Chapter Seven: Starting Over | 81

to the inmates. I always felt that they heard what I had to say, and maybe it changed a few lives. Lori and I had really gotten into the Bible and were doing a Bible study with some friends. Lori was also teaching Sunday school at church, so it was all positive stuff.

It was time for the trip to Hawaii, and we flew from Boston to San Francisco, then Oahu. It was a long flight, and we landed in the evening. We had a hotel on Waikiki Beach, and it was just magical. We lost our luggage, and so the airline gave us a few bucks to get some things, but we just didn't care. We went out and walked the beach under the moonlight, which was perfect. The next morning, I got Lori up, and we headed out to go climb Diamond Head Volcano. We got there and started climbing the stairs. If you have ever been there, you know it was a huge climb, at least for us. We made it to the top, hit our knees, and thanked God for that beauty. It was just breathtaking! We climbed back down and were pretty much wiped out by the time we got back to the room. We ordered out and decided to rest. When we woke up the next morning, we could hardly move! Our legs just wouldn't work; they were so sore! But we pushed on!

Then reality set in, and we realized we had lost our luggage! Now, I can live with a pair of shorts, a t-shirt, and flip-flops, but not so my wife! She needs stuff, and all her stuff got lost. This was like hanging a piece of chicken in front of an alligator. Lori went on a quest to find our luggage, and I lived in the moment and stayed out of her way. They ended up finding it about four days into the trip and got it to us, so Lori calmed down, and we started exploring. There was a huge outdoor marketplace across the street from our hotel, so we went to check it out. There was this guy with a bunch of oysters in a tank, and a sign said, "See if you can get a pearl." Lori got all excited and bought one, and the guy cut it open. There were two pearls in it, and he was acting really amazed, which, in turn, got Lori incredibly excited. I just stood back, watching it all take place. The guy was like, "Oh my gosh, that never happens; this is extremely rare!" Lori believed him, and the

82 | A Fall to Grace

guy said, "For a small price, we can make a set of earrings for you." She was just about to say yes when I pulled her aside to tell her it was a scam. She was so mad, and she took the pearls and walked away. We let the next unsuspecting couple try it!

We went all over Oahu, but the best part was Pearl Harbor. We did the whole experience. It was just surreal to stand above the battleship Arizona and pray for those lost souls. We spent four days in Oahu and then flew to Maui. We rented a convertible Mustang and headed to our hotel. When we got there, we upgraded to a bungalow on the shore, and it was perfect. Every morning I would get up at daylight and go snorkeling right in front of our place. It was cool, with a bunch of lava formations underwater and tons of fish. The water was crystal clear. I felt so close to God there. We had a friend from Maine who had a condo on the island. He was a seafood dealer from back home, so we went to Lahaina to his place to visit. He had a beautiful view overlooking the bay. I figured I was in the wrong business; I should have been dealing lobsters, not catching them! He took us on a tour around the small town, and the history was so interesting! The whaling boats out of New Bedford, MA, used to sail all the way over there to fish and go into Lahaina to get provisions before heading back. Now, that must have been quite a trip! We also ran into Steven Tyler from Aerosmith on Main Street. Our friend also took us to an AA meeting on the beach, and I celebrated six years of sobriety. I will always remember that!

We drove all over the island of Maui. We went to Hana, which is on the back side of Haleakala Mountain. You must drive this really narrow winding road, basically on the side of cliffs, with hairpin turns. You must beep the horn to let oncoming cars know that you are approaching the turn! It was unreal and beautiful! I had done a lot of research about the island and wanted to visit as many waterfalls as we could, so that is what we did! There was one time we drove down a dirt road by a couple of houses, and in a couple of minutes, a Jeep pulled out in front of us and stopped us. There were four guys in it, and they got out and came up to my window and asked where I was going and said it was private property. I wanted to give the guy a hard time, but Lori was giving me the evil eye, so I kept quiet and turned around! We still saw a bunch of waterfalls and ended up in Hana, which is a small farm town with these huge cliffs. It was just breathtaking! We both decided that when we die, that was where we'd want our ashes scattered. We also drove up to Mount Haleakala, which takes you through about five different climates. The top is like a moonscape, and it was quite cold up there! That was so awesome. We ended our trip at a huge luau, which was impressive, and the food was great. We left the islands with renewed minds and spirits.

Michael on Criehaven Island ME

Michael and Lori 2003

Deck full of scallops

Michael, Billy-son, Bob-brother

Michael and Lori Wedding

Lobster Family

Lori Lee Spruce Head ME, Pt. 1

Lori Lee Spruce Head ME, Pt. 2

Chapter Eight:
Life Gets Real

How long, Lord? Will you forget me forever? How long will you hide your face from me? How long must I wrestle with my thoughts and day after day have sorrow in my heart? How long will my enemy triumph over me?

Psalm 13:1–2

After that, I started doing gear work and put the boat over at the end of March, a little early, but I was hungry. Billy got through his first year and came home, Lori was back at her job at the bank, and all was good. As things were starting to look up, the engine blew up in the boat, so we had to take out another loan to replace it, and again Lori stepped up to save the day. We were further in the hole, and I could tell Lori was stressed out. We got the engine in the boat and put it back over in time for the first run of lobsters. We were starting to do pretty well, so I hired one of my friends to go with me. He was really experienced, and we made a good team.

As summer rolled on, I decided to take Lori on a trip to Boston. She loved the museums, and we got a room right on the harbor. We had a great time, except my hips were really starting to bother me. We decided to go see a specialist when we got home. We made an appointment with an orthopedic surgeon in Portland. He took some X-rays and said that both my hips were shot and needed to be replaced. Thank God Lori had good insurance. We figured that I would have them both done at the end of the lobster season. But I decided that I needed something stronger for pain, and the doctor gave me a prescription for Vicodin. Not the smartest thing I have ever done. Lori was upset that I had gotten the script, but as a good addict always does, I talked my way into it. Lobsters came hard, so I was hauling like crazy and taking more pain pills because they gave me energy.

Billy went back for his sophomore year, and I finished up with my best year lobstering thus far. Just before I took my traps up, my friend Pete came over to the house and said we needed to start taking our Able Bodied (AB) Seaman classes so we could ship out and make money in the winter. This sounded like a really good idea, so that's what we did. The classes were held at Maine Maritime Academy, so Pete drove us up every day, and we completed the course and got our AB tickets. Right after that, I had my first hip surgery, and they put me on OxyContin for the pain. I went home that day and started physical therapy, and four weeks later, I had my second surgery. The problem was that I had been on painkillers for about three months and was totally addicted again. I knew how much pain getting off them was going to be, but I kept getting more. After my second surgery, I started weaning myself off the pills and finally got clean in six weeks.

I got a job for the winter on a tugboat out of Boothbay Harbor that was working in Virginia with a big dredging company. I got on the boat in Providence, RI. I was sore and probably still withdrawing, but I pushed through it anyway. I had never worked on a tugboat, so it was all new, and it was really frustrating until one of the captains took me under his wing. He showed me so many different things about the job it actually started to be fun. We took the tug to a job in Baltimore, MD, and as we were working, one of the union reps, named Red, came aboard and asked me if I had a union card. I didn't, and he convinced me to join the union. I didn't know how important that day was until a few years later. This type of work was just a part-time job until June or so; then, I was going back to lobstering. We were working fourteen days on and seven days off. We lived aboard the boat, tending

90 | A Fall to Grace

these big scows. They were filling these scows with mud from two big bucket dredges we had out in the Chesapeake Bay. We would pick up the scows and bring them into an unloader we had next to this island that we were making. They would pump the mud out, and then we would take the empty ones back to the dredges to be filled again. This was a stable job with good benefits. I kept clean during my tugging days and was feeling pretty good about myself.

I finished up with tugging in the late spring, and the union was pretty disappointed because they didn't want me to quit, but I did, and I headed home to start setting traps. Billy had gotten through another year of college, and Lori was healthy and doing well at her job. She was happy about how I was doing, so all was good on the home front. We were doing well lobstering, but I was still having some pain, or so I thought, in my hips and legs, most likely because I didn't follow the doctor's orders on my physical therapy. I was dealing with it until, one day, I decided to go to the clinic and get some pain meds because that's what my addictive mind was telling me, not thinking of what it would do to my wife, son, or business. So, I did it and kept doing it through the fall. I was taking everything, from pain meds to muscle relaxers. It got so bad at the end of the fall that Lori had to drive me down to the dock so I could tell my sternman I couldn't go because I was too messed up.

My wife had every right to kick me to the curb. We had promised each other to remain clean and sober when we got married. She stood by me and told me that I needed rehab. She set up an interview with a twenty-eight-day rehab in Florida and said if I didn't take up my gear and go, then she would leave me. So, I headed to Florida and detox. When I got off the plane, a person picked me up at the airport and dropped me off at the detox. So started yet another four-day withdrawal that was not pleasant. They took me to rehab on the fifth day, and I got to see my therapist. Her name was Joan, and she was a really tough woman. The first thing she said to me was, "Do you know how much you are hurting your family?" This really caught me off guard. I broke

Chapter Eight: Life Gets Real | 91

down and cried for a while, and she told me to stop being so self-ish and to get my act together and get clean. I told her that I was going to do just that, which was a lie because, deep down, I was still thinking that I could take pain pills and work. What a selfish, self-centered jerk I was!

We did a bunch of classes and groups and got homework for each one. Being the overachiever, I would do my homework right away and pass it to Joan, but she would always send it back for a redo. I used to get *sooo* mad! Today, I realize what she was doing; I just wasn't willing to change. My biggest problem had always been my ego, and it was proving to be a huge obstacle in my recovery. I wouldn't let go and surrender to my addiction. I wanted to control it, which just wasn't possible. I lied my way through the program and called my wife to get me a ticket home because I was clean and sober. My counselors were telling me that I wasn't ready, but what did they know? I had to get to work and make money, not sit there and listen to their psychobabble. I flew home and promised my wife that I would go to lots of AA meetings, and all would be good. "Love is bliss."

I did hit lots of meetings, but my heart wasn't into it. I was more focused on getting my boat and traps ready to go for another season. We started early that year, so it was a struggle to make money at first. As the season moved into summer, things got better. Billy finally decided on a major in economics and decided that he wanted to finish in four years so that he could get a job. That was a good thing! My relationship with Lori had changed. She had lost trust in me, and I could feel it, so I threw myself into work that much more.

Lori had a great job and had become assistant manager of a local bank branch close to home. Billy was doing well lobstering, plus he had a great job with another fisherman, so he was all set. I was catching loads of lobsters. On the outside, as a family, we looked like we were doing great, but underneath, things were anything but good. Billy went off to start his senior year in college.

92 | A Fall to Grace

I was so proud of him for getting that far, being a high school dropout myself. Now, you would think that with all this positive stuff in my life, I would be riding high on the horse, but that is when addiction creeps into your life. You let down your guard, and it will kill you!

I started buying a few pills off the street so my wife wouldn't know, and before long, I was full-blown again. I justified it by this being my biggest lobster year ever. We were getting 1,000-pound hauls every week, and I was working like a maniac. I couldn't hide the money trail, so I started buying methadone from a few of my so-called friends because it lasted longer, and I was hiding it all over the house. Lori knew, but she loved me and didn't want to leave me. I can't imagine how much it hurt her to stay, but she did. I finished the year up in a grand fashion and decided to take Lori on a trip to St. Lucia to mend our relationship.

We flew down, and I didn't bring any pills, so I was withdrawing the whole trip. It really stunk, but I had to do it to show her I was okay. What a lie! I'm sure she knew. My screwed-up thoughts were all over the place! St. Lucia was a really beautiful place, and we did have some fun, but I ruined it with my addiction and my lack of connection with God. All I could think of was getting home and getting my boat and gear ready. We flew home, and I had been clean for ten days, but as soon as I could, I got more methadone.

Billy graduated that spring, and it was just so unbelievable to watch him march with his class. I was so proud of him! He got an internship with Senator Susan Collins in Washington, DC, the following fall, so that part of my life was great. He was on his way to greater things!

As I was doing gear work one day, I got a call from one of my fishermen friends, and he said he had some heroin. Now, I swore I would never do dope again after prison, but I said yes, and he showed up at my shop with dope and a needle. I didn't use the

Chapter Eight: Life Gets Real | 93

needle, but I knew deep down that was next…I had sunk as low as I could go. My sternman, who was a friend, showed up the day we were putting the boat over and walked up to me and said that he couldn't go fishing with me until I got some help for my drug addiction. This floored me, but he said that I had been nodding out while working and that I really needed help. I got defensive, but I knew he was right. He said if I got clean, he would continue to go with me. I sat on my trap trailer for about a half hour and decided to come clean with my wife. I went inside and told her what had just happened. I was expecting sympathy, but she got really quiet, and then she said to get out. She had had enough. This really freaked me out, and I felt really lost. I knew something had to change, so I drove to the local hospital and checked into the detox.

I can't tell you how empty I felt knowing that I had let down my family. Worse was the fact that all the people who said I would fail were right. I started another journey in detox with less hope than I've ever had. A few of my AA friends showed up to try to help me, but all my fishing buddies stayed away. After a couple of days of shaking and baking, Lori showed up, and they had an intervention with me. The detox center offered methadone and Suboxone treatments, which meant that I would be on this stuff for life. I was about to give up and just accept that way of life, but my wife was not going to stay with me if I did. I called the rehab in Florida, where I had previously gone, and asked them to accept me once more, and they said yes. Lori just said we would see if our relationship would make it.

I had a couple more days to detox before I headed to Florida, and I asked if they could give me Suboxone to help with my withdrawal. That night I was waiting in line to get my fix, and as I got to the window, the nurse said that I had a choice. If I took the Suboxone, I would have to stay there because the rehab would not accept me if I was taking any maintenance medications. This was totally God giving me a choice! I was at a fork in the road. I prayed for direction, and God answered.

94 | A Fall to Grace

Chapter Nine:
Darkest Before The Dawn

Turn to me and be gracious to me, for I am lonely and afflicted.
Relieve the troubles of my heart and free me from my anguish.
Look on my affliction and my distress and take away all my sins.
See how numerous are my enemies and how fiercely they hate me!
Guard my life and rescue me; do not let me be put to shame, for
I take refuge in you. May integrity and uprightness protect me,
because my hope, Lord, is in you.

Psalm 25:16–21

On Easter morning, 2011, I boarded the plane, and off to
Florida I went. To the same rehab that I had left a few years before,
telling them that I was cured of my addictions and that I would
never be back. I landed at the airport, and they met me at the gate
and took me right to rehab; no detox this time. I got unpacked and
was told to go and meet with my counselor, who, of course, was
Joan. This time she was meaner than I remembered. The first thing
she said was, "You are probably not going to get clean." Then she
proceeded to tell me how much I had hurt my wife and son. She
had seen hundreds of addicts like me who told her what she wanted to hear. She had seen many addicts die. She really gave me an
earful! I left there feeling so dirty and lost. I can't even explain it.

The first thing Joan did was take my phone and not allow me
to contact Lori for at least a month. I was so angry that I almost
left, but I did lots of praying and stayed because I knew deep down
this was my last shot at any kind of life. I missed Lori and Billy so
much, but my ego was still in control, and I was faking my way
through, and Joan knew it. I had been there for about three weeks,

and they had this thing called family week where they would bring the family in to have them tell their struggles with your addiction and to see the progress you had been making. I was really upset because I still wasn't allowed to contact my family, so there was no family week for me. I was sitting in a group on the first day of family week, and one of the techs came in and asked me to go with him. As we were headed across the parking lot, I realized we were going to the family room, and I knew Lori was there. When I saw her, I just started crying, but she was acting differently. There were a bunch of other families there, and the head counselor was there, and she was extremely tough. She started grilling me, and everybody started going at me, telling me that I didn't deserve Lori and what a jerk I had been. Then Lori looked at me and said she wanted a separation and that she was going to sell the lobster business because everything was in her name, and she didn't want to lose her good credit. I was just stunned and speechless, so I got up, and the counselor told me to leave. I went to the office and said that I wanted my stuff, that I was done. I was sure that Lori didn't mean it and that she would take me home. As I was sitting in the parking lot waiting for something to happen, it dawned on me that Lori had left by herself, and I was all alone. I broke down and was just sobbing like never before. Everything deep inside of me was coming out, and I was just begging God to fix me. Just as I was praying, a couple of young guys I didn't like came up to me and put their arms around me; they picked me up and said they wouldn't let me leave. They said I should stay and start truly working on the program. By the grace of God, that day saved my life!

I not only got serious about the program, but I started some real conversations with God, and He started answering me. A bunch of my friends and my son called me and told me that Lori was selling the lobster business and asked what was going on. I told them the truth: that I had relapsed and broken her trust, so she had every right to sell it. When speaking to my son, I just said it was okay, that I trusted that God has another purpose for me

96 | A Fall to Grace

other than lobstering. I explained that the lobstering business had always been poison to me. I told him that I loved him with all my heart. I don't know if anyone, including my son, understood my decision, but I was done with lobstering, and it was time to see what God had in store.

Thus, started my true journey into faith, recovery, and a deep love for God. My thinking had been so screwed up. I had to put God first, my recovery second, and my family third because if I wasn't clean and sober, I was absolutely no good to anyone, period! I started really working with Joan and not rushing my assignments, plus I started going to church and reading the Bible. I was so hungry for all of it, no matter what was going to happen to me.

I finally got the courage to call Lori and tell her that I loved her and that I wanted to spend the rest of my life with her. I also said that we should sell everything and move to Florida and see what happened. To my surprise, she agreed, and so after a few more weeks in the program, I flew home and put everything up for sale. There is a saying in AA that you must give up your old playground and playmates if you want to stay clean. This time, I was listening to that advice!

We had a couple of extra acres with our trailer that we decided to sell. As I was getting ready to put a "For Sale" sign up, one of our neighbors came out of his house and immediately bought it! Now, that was another God-moment telling me we were making the right decision. Our boat got sold to a local young fisherman, and all the gear (traps and buoys) went quickly. We rented the trailer to a friend who had gone through a divorce and needed a place. We were able to pay off all our bills and still had a few bucks left to get set up in Florida. Billy was able to help us drive all our stuff down, and so we left the little fishing village for what I was sure was the last time. I drove the big U-Haul truck, Billy was in our pick-up, all loaded down, and Lori was in the minivan with the dog and cat and all the fragile items. We were doing well until we got to NYC, then we got a little turned around. This was before we owned

Chapter Nine: Darkest Before The Dawn | 97

smartphones! We got back on track and headed south on I-95. It took us three days to get to the house we rented in Pompano Beach, Florida. Thank God Billy was with us to help us unload!

Our rental was an older, typical Florida-style house with a nice fenced-in backyard, but a couple of blocks over was the hood, so we didn't venture very far on our walks. We both found jobs, Lori with a big bank, and I got a job with the maintenance department of the rehab that I went to. This was really my first job on land, so it was an adventure! Things were going well.

We were starting to save money, and we had started attending this megachurch in Coral Springs. When we started at this church, there were around 8,000 people who attended, and now it is about 25,000. It was just crazy how many people were hungry for Jesus! During the first service we went to, the pastor drove down the aisle on a John Deere tractor, and the worship music seemed like a rock concert. We just loved it! A few weeks later, we were there with another couple, and the pastor said, "If you've never given your heart to Jesus, why would you go one more day without Him?" Then he explained that a full water baptism was the outward sign of our inward decision. I looked at Lori, got up, grabbed her hand, and the other couple looked at us and followed us down the front, and we all got fully dunked in the water. The feeling was unbelievable when I came up from the water! I felt free! Both of us had tears of joy coming down our faces.

Just to give you an example of how crazy it can be to live in Florida, one day, our dog came up to the back door and had a water bottle in her mouth. As I got it from her, I noticed it had been used to smoke crack. Lori and I decided to throw it out. A few days later, the dog had another one. I started going around the fenced-in backyard area, which had a bunch of bamboo growing, and it was quite dense. I found about twenty-five cans in a pile next to the fence where our neighbor lived. I grabbed a bunch of them and went to their house to confront the owner. He blamed his son, so we let it go, but as I got to know the guy, I realized

98 | A Fall to Grace

he was definitely the addict. It was at that point that we started looking for another place to live. I tried to talk to this guy who, on the outside, looked great. He had a nice house, pool, beautiful boat, and good job, but a very big secret! He denied any addiction problems. There is an old saying that you can lead a horse to water, but you can't make it drink. In addition to "crack dude" on the one side, we also had "cat lady" on the other side. This lady had like fifty cats living in her house, and they would come over the fence, and our dog would go crazy.

My job was not that fun; for example, one day, my boss asked me to go to one of the rooms and clean the bathroom. What I didn't know was that the toilet had backed up, and raw sewage had blown all over the walls. It was so gross. I cleaned it up but decided to call my union and get back into the shipping industry. I gave the rehab a two-week notice, and the union set me up with a job out of Fort Pierce, FL, on a tugboat.

I started earning good money as a deckhand, but the company that I started working for had a lot of drug and alcohol use. I decided that for my sobriety, I needed to leave the company. I called the union, and they put me on another tugboat working out of St. Petersburg, FL. This was a cool job because the captain I was working for started pushing me to get my captain's license. I had plenty of sea time, but I had to take a test, and I was a little afraid of failure.

We eventually found a two-bed, two-bath older double-wide, completely renovated, in a fifty-five-plus retirement community. This was the first place I had purchased on my own since the house in Portland, ME, with my ex-wife. This time I didn't need Lori's signature. I had a secure job with great benefits, so I got to cover Lori's health insurance, which was huge for me. Finally, I was taking care of my family, not the other way around. I kept working in St. Pete until the job was over, and I got offered a job with another dredging company out of Southport, NC. I was hired to work as a deckhand for a big cutterhead dredge. This is a floating dredge with a cutterhead that is connected to a ladder,

Chapter Nine: Darkest Before The Dawn | 99

and they move the ladder down to the sea floor. The dredge has huge engines, which turn the cutterhead, and this churns the sand or cuts the rock, which, in turn, is sucked up with pumps and either moved through a pipe to a beach or to a spider barge, which scows tie up to, and the sand is moved into them until they are full. Then tugboats replace them with empty scows and take the full ones out to be dumped in special areas. There is a lot to it, and these guys are just amazing to work with! We work in some treacherous weather, but we get it done.

Chapter Ten:
Never Too Late For A New Career

For you, Lord, have delivered me from death,
my eyes from tears, my feet from stumbling, that I may
walk before the Lord in the land of the living.

Psalm 116:8–9

Being a deckhand was fun, but I started watching these crew boats coming back and forth and decided that was what I wanted to do. I finally went to Sea School on my time off and got my official Coast-Guard-approved captain's license. I let the union know that I got my license but getting on a crew boat as captain was rare. A job finally came up, and I put my name in for it, but one of the captain's sons got the job. I went back for one more hitch and was having a hard time getting along with the crew, so I asked the union to find me something else. The union was not happy, but a couple of weeks later, I got hired as a captain for another company doing a job up in the Hudson River by Glens Falls, NY. This job was a little different because we stayed on the job the whole season. We got double subsistence, and we only worked six days a week. I got up there in early September, so it was starting to get chilly, but it was so beautiful. The leaves were changing colors, and we were working in old historical towns. We were doing a cleanup of the upper Hudson River because a big company had been dumping PCBs into the river for decades. When I got there, the crew boat I was supposed to run was broken down, so they put me as a deckhand on a small push boat. I was getting my captain's pay, so at first, it was good, but after two weeks, I was still a deckhand. I started making calls and finally got a boat. I had never worked on a river, and we were running these pontoon boats with twin outboards, so there was quite a learning curve, but I caught on pretty quickly. There were locks we had to go through on the river. A lock is a manmade passage around some obstacle, like a waterfall. We would go into one, they would shut the gate, and if we were going upriver, they would fill it up, and if we were going down the river, they would empty it out. All we had to do was tie up and wait until they gave us the green light. It started to be really fun after the first couple of times! We had five dredges scattered over ten miles of river. I would relieve the night operator at around 5 AM, do a crew run at 6 AM, then come back to the dock and let the other crew get off. Then I would do whatever else they needed during the day. The dredges were a bunch of Flexi-floats put together with a Conbox for the crew and an excavator for the digging. We would fill scows with the muck on the bottom of the river, and small tugs would move them around. Once they were full, the tugs would bring them to an unloading dock where the contaminated material would be processed and shipped out.

My wife came up to visit at the beginning of October, and we stayed at this beautiful bed and breakfast in Schuylerville, a quaint little town on the Hudson River. We went all over exploring and seeing the sights. We went to where the Battle of Saratoga took place. It was also apple picking season, and there was a type called Honeycrisp that was to die for! There were farm stands and little diners, and they had apple pancakes, apple pies, apple ice cream...well, you get the picture. It was apple mania! It was a nice change from Florida.

It was starting to get cool at night, and we had these see-through plastic covers that we put up to keep the wind out, but it was still chilly! I started working nights, which didn't have a lot of runs, so I got to cruise up and down the Hudson and see how beautiful the night sky was, full of stars! We were getting close to shutting down for the season because the river would freeze, and it had started snowing occasionally. I was wearing a fully insulat-

102 | A Fall to Grace

ed suit by then and still freezing! Eventually, I got laid off, and I packed up and headed home to Florida for some heat!

Almost as soon as I got home and unpacked, the union called and offered me a job in Miami for a couple of weeks. I really didn't want to go, but I prayed about it and decided to take it. The job was working for our biggest dredging contractor; however, the boat was a small survey boat, which I had never run before. The commute from our house was about fifty minutes, so I didn't have to rent a hotel room, and I would be able to be home every night. The company was running a few boats out of Sea Isle Marina, right in the heart of Miami. I had always dreamed of running a boat in Biscayne Bay after watching *Miami Vice* on television when I was younger. I used to love that show, and now, here I was! The boat was thirty feet and aluminum, so it was heavy, with a lot of equipment. It was really only big enough for two people.

We were doing a job over by the Tuttle Bridge, and we had a large area fenced in with these turbidity curtains. We were filling in a huge underwater hole that had been dug when the bridge was built. Our company would bring scows full of sand into the area and dump them, and then I would go in and survey the area to get the depths. The Army Corps of Engineers oversaw the project, so we were under strict regulations. I always had one engineer on the boat with me, and his name was Jay. We had so much fun doing our jobs and enjoying each day. We would go up the Miami River and stop at this place and grab lunch. It was always an adventure on the bay, especially on weekends and holidays, when the public would be out on the water. People were out in force! Sunseekers were on yachts, power boats, Jet Skis, and kayaks; it was very stressful to work in the middle of it!

I was hired full-time after the first two weeks and worked 3,400 hours during my first year in Miami. The money was really good. When I got out of jail, I owed so much money, and Lori supported me most of the time until I got back on my feet. But now, we had finally paid off all of my back debt, and I was starting

Chapter Ten: Never Too Late For A New Career | 103

to repair my credit. Lori was taking some classes in the health field and was working at a supplement store. She loved being healthy.

There were some pretty colorful people living in our fifty-five-plus community. Our next-door neighbor was this old dude from Massachusetts with one leg, whom we called P. Diddy. He was very cynical and complained about everything, but we became friends. I used to love to visit him and listen to him. I think we brightened his days.

After about a year and a half, the project manager of the Miami job called and asked if I wanted to move over to the crew boat division because they were almost done with the job and the surveying, so I said yes. I had never run a twin screw boat other than the twin outboards up in the Hudson, but I told him I could do it. On my first day, after getting done with the crew run, I spent the day teaching myself how to use both engines to navigate and back up to the dredges and docks. I also asked a lot of questions, and the other captains helped me out. Within a week, I was pretty good and started to relax a bit. The problem in Miami was the amount of small boat traffic all day and night. All of our equipment had lights, but people just didn't pay attention and were either running aground because they picked the wrong side of the dredge to pass by, or they would bounce off our equipment because they were drinking a little too much! I spent hours trying to keep boaters out of our danger zone, but on holidays it was just crazy. Hundreds of novice boaters were just going every which way. It was still a very cool place to be, though. I surveyed the shore of Fisher Island, where the super-rich stayed, although I never saw many people outside, and we never knew what we would see on South Beach! I did see a few model shoots, and they filmed a few movies with boat and car chase scenes while I was there.

I had been working in Miami for a couple of years, and we were starting to really come ahead in our finances. I was starting to get homesick, so over the course of the next year, we started looking at houses up in Maine. I really loved working in Miami, but I was driving an hour each way every day in the second worst traffic in the country, and it was wearing me down. The job was winding down, and it sounded like the company was going to haul the boat out for a few months to work on it, which meant a layoff for me, so we ramped up our search for a house back in Maine.

Billy was doing really well in Washington, DC. He and another kid from Maine were sharing rent together. We got to see him on holidays, and once in a while, we would fly up to DC to see him. We were so proud of him, and he enjoyed his independence.

A friend of ours was a real estate agent in Camden, ME, so we contacted him, and he really narrowed our search to six to seven houses. Lori flew up in the middle of the winter, and she fell in love with this place in Cushing. It was a small farm on thirty acres of wooded land with a nice barn, and it was close to the water. Cushing was on the next peninsula over from where I had grown up, so it was close, but not too close. We made an offer, and the owners took it, so we signed the papers and bought the place. We sold the double-wide immediately, so we started another moving journey across the country. We sold the place in Florida with everything in it and bought the house in Cushing fully furnished, so this made the move a bit easier.

Before I got out of Florida, I got a call from the union asking me to stop in Savannah, GA. They had decided to keep the boat that I was working on running, and they were sending it to Savannah. I rented a room in a house on Wilmington Island, close to Tybee Island, which was where we were working. I just loved Savannah; it was old, with trees full of Spanish moss hanging from the branches and the people were really nice. It reminded me of what the Old South was all about. We were working four weeks on and two weeks off, so I was flying out of Savannah to Portland, ME. I had been there a couple of hitches and had noticed that my chest was a little tight, but I figured I was just out of shape.

When I got home, I got up early one morning and decided to

Chapter Ten: Never Too Late For A New Career | 105

try to figure out the southern borderline of our property. The land was heavily wooded, so as I stepped off the back porch, something told me to grab some orange tape to mark my trail. This was something that I had never done. As the dog and I were walking out in the woods, I started to feel something hot in both my arms and flowing down to my hands. I started getting really dizzy, and the first thing that I wanted to do was to sit down and rest. Then I felt that God spoke to me, and I was filled with a sense of urgency to get back to the house. I realized that I was way out in the woods. How would I find my way out fast? As panic started to set in, I turned around and saw the path I had marked with the orange tape and knew why I had taken it! I half jogged out of the woods, up the field, into the house, and up the stairs.

My wife took one look at me and asked if I was okay. All I could say was "heart attack." She put me in the car and got me to the local hospital. They did some tests, put me in an ambulance, and sent me to Portland. I needed a double bypass! After surgery, I was in the recovery unit, and a very strange thing happened. I woke up, or at least I thought I did, and it was totally dark, but there was something coming to get me, and it wasn't good. I could almost see it, and I guess I was screaming, "Get away from me." I woke up with the nurse standing over me. It really freaked me out! The doctor came in a little while later and said that one of my main arteries had collapsed and if I had stopped to rest, I would have died! He also looked at me and said, "God's not done with you yet!" I almost fell out of bed because then I knew that God had me get that orange tape!

I was in the hospital for a couple of days, and I told the doctor that I only wanted enough pain pills to get me home, and that is what I got. I was in so much pain, but the idea of going through rehab again just made me tough it out. Over the next few days, a few of my friends stopped by. I got into physical therapy right away and really pushed it. I went back to work in ten weeks, and it was probably a little early, but I felt okay.

106 | A Fall to Grace

The job was winding down in Savannah, and I was offered a crew boat in Palm Beach. When I got there, the boat was hauled out, and it was a mess. I put in three weeks getting it ready to sail; I'm not even sure why they brought it down. The bright side was that I got to stay at a friend's newly built house. He had been one of the people who had really helped me in drug rehab. It was great staying with him and his wife. My wife and son got to come down for Christmas because my friends went up north to visit their family. We had their house for the holidays! I will forever be grateful to those two people who showed me real kindness and generosity.

This job was getting close to being over, and I was offered a job in New Jersey on one of the bigger crew boats. The funny thing about this boat was back when I was trying to be a captain for another dredge company in Atlantic City, this crew boat was tied up at the same dock that we were using, and I remember saying that I would love to run a boat like that someday. And God put it in my path!

This job was right by Atlantic City, so you could see all the casinos rising up from offshore. I learned from one of our runners, who grew up there, about the history of Atlantic City. We would go out to lunch, and he would give me tours and tell me stories of all the mobsters who controlled the city and all the crazy things that happened. The history was wild, and now the city was falling apart, with a lot of drugs and homelessness. All this was happening in a city that had so much glitter!

By this time, Billy had gotten a promotion within the government and had gotten a nice raise, so that was awesome. He was deputy director of the National Resource Committee, working on oceans, power, and water. He was starting to travel a bit for his job. He basically got to fly around the world a couple of times and visit many different islands and countries. I was so proud of him for sticking it out during the tough times in DC. If he had stayed in Maine, he probably would have never had these opportunities. I am grateful for Lori pushing him to go to college. In the end, it was

Chapter Ten: Never Too Late For A New Career | 107

all his great work ethic and personality that made people want him on their team. It breaks my heart that I wasn't present very much for the first fifteen years of his life. This is something that I will never get back. If I could offer any advice, it would be: if you have children, please take the time to nurture and love them!

With that job done, we got orders to head up to Philadelphia for our next job. We docked the boat in Chester, which is a few miles from the center of the city and is a pretty rough place. I got a room on the New Jersey side of the river because I figured I would get killed on the Chester side. When I was on nights and had to drive out of the dock, I had to drive through some really dangerous neighborhoods, and I wouldn't stop for anything. Just a little scared, I guess!

We were blasting rock with a specialized drill barge, which meant we would drill a bunch of holes in the rock under the water, then pack them with explosives and blast it. I would do crew runs, then provide security while explosives were being used. In other words, I would keep the river clear of traffic. It was interesting to watch. First, there would be a countdown, then the blast with a big boom would send a geyser of water up in the air. Then we would come in and survey the area to make sure that there weren't any high spots that ships could hit. After that, we would bring in one of our bucket dredges and dig the rock up and fill it into barges to be towed down the river to an artificial reef we were making off the Maryland coast. I had been watching our survey vessels work for quite some time, and I really wanted to get on another one, but again, it was a tough nut to crack. They had one captain who worked days, and most of these captains had been there for years. I did have the inside scoop on who was coming and going, so if I saw an opportunity, I would grab it!

I was driving back and forth to Philly from Maine, which was a stretch. During this time, Lori and I had gotten involved in a church plant starting in our local area. We had been praying about this since we left Florida. It was in a local movie theater, and atten-

108 | A Fall to Grace

dance started to grow, which was exciting to watch. We went from twenty people to one hundred fifty people in about a month. We had a great pastor who was on fire for God, or so it seemed. Lori decided to leave her job at the bank and do the Lord's work in our new church. As the church started to grow in membership, we needed a bigger space. There was this Baptist church in the area that was struggling, and they decided that we would merge. Things seemed to be on the fast track, and when we took over the older church, everything changed overnight. The new church started selling all its possessions, like the organ, stained glass windows, art, and historical items. It was explained that these things drove people away, and we were a new creation. Then out of nowhere, the pastor decided to sell his house and leave the church without telling anyone! This all happened in about eighteen months. It was so confusing to think God was leading us, but looking back, we realize that human egos were getting in the way of God. We were really hurt by all of this, especially my wife, so we walked away from this church, as did a lot of others. We had pretty much destroyed a church that had been active for over one hundred fifty years just to take over their building. I bought into this nightmare and am so sorry for the older people who had their church pulled out from under them. Needless to say, Lori and I won't be doing that again. We thought this was our calling, but after a time of reflection, we both realized that it was more about us getting the praise and glory rather than giving it to God. It was a hard lesson to learn.

The job in Philly was going well, and it looked like we could be there a few years, so we started renovating the house in Maine with a new kitchen, a new heating system, and adding a bunch of stonework on the outside. We thought we would stay there forever. It was a beautiful and special property.

One day I decided that I needed a Harley-Davidson and my neighbor just happened to have a couple, so I went over and talked him out of one. I didn't have a motorcycle license, so that was next on my agenda. I took the class and passed, so I began riding. I had decided that everything I was to do from then on had to glorify God, so I joined a Christian bikers club and started riding for Jesus. It was really uplifting. We set up booths at some racing events, where we got to do the opening prayer. We would pray over other riders at gas stations. We were always looking for ways to help people get to God.

The job in Philly lasted two years, and then I got the call to bring the boat to Savannah. So one of the other captains and I headed that way. We went through the Delaware Canal and stopped in the Solomon Islands for the night. This was a neat place on the upper Chesapeake Bay. We left at first light and made it through Norfolk, VA, into the Intercoastal Waterway (ICW), and got to Coinjock, NC. This was a little town with a marina on the ICW, and it was famous for its prime rib meal in the local restaurant. Twenty-two ounces of pure pleasure! We got stuck in Coinjock for four days because the wind came up, and when the wind blows over a certain speed, the bridges won't open. We rented a place right on the water, and the boat was tied up right out front. My wife was going to meet us on the next leg of the journey and drive my truck down to Savannah.

The weather finally broke, so we left, and it was still a little breezy but had let down quite a bit. There were a few large bays we had to cross, and it was still choppy, but the boat was a fifty-five-footer and handled the seas well. We arrived in Morehead City, NC, around 6 PM, and Lori was there, waiting for us at the marina. We rented a couple of rooms and went out to dinner. Morehead City is a great fishing town with good seafood restaurants. The weather was good when we got up the next day, so we headed to the next stop, which was Georgetown, SC. We got there about 4:30 PM, and again Lori was there waiting. Georgetown is a little mill town with a bunch of unique shops and restaurants. We ate and got rooms right up from the marina and turned in for the night. We got up early and headed for Charleston after

110 | A Fall to Grace

breakfast. As I was checking the engine room, I discovered one of our shafts was leaking, so we turned around and went back to the marina. It was a rubber seal, and we needed to pull the shaft to fix it, which meant we had to haul the boat out, so we decided to patch it up the best we could, grab an extra sump pump, and head for Charleston. We made it there around 8 PM and tied the boat up at the Charleston Harbor Marina. This was a huge marina, where Lori met us; we got rooms, ate, and made some calls to figure out what to do next. Our mechanics wanted us to bring the boat to Thunderbolt Marina in Savannah and haul it out to fix the problem. The next morning, we left Charleston at daylight and got to the marina around 1 PM. We had the boat hauled out to be repaired. Lori picked us up, and we got rooms where we would be relieved and another crew would take over. We gave Bill, the other captain, a ride to the airport, and Lori and I went to Tybee Island near Savannah for a few days of vacation. We got up the next day, which happened to be St. Paddy's Day, and it was already crazy on the beach! We went into Savannah and walked around and shopped. We sat on the bench where Forrest Gump talked about chocolates, walked through some neat parks in town, and ended up eating a delicious meal at The Cotton Exchange, which was right on the river. We were in love with Savannah so much that we started looking at properties because that's just what we do! It's kind of an inside joke.

I worked out of Savannah for a few hitches, and then we were sent to Charleston, and we were told it would be a long job. Lori started looking for a place to rent on Mount Pleasant, a section of Charleston. We found a great one-bed, one-bath condo for a good price, so we rented it and put minimal furniture in it. The idea was that Lori could come down in the winter, and we could spend the cold weather months in Charleston together. We found a great church and also found a few good recovery meetings in the area. Charleston is such a unique city with tons of history and tons of restaurants. Yes, we started looking at properties, and now you

Chapter Ten: Never Too Late For A New Career | 111

know the joke, we look at properties everywhere we go!

I remember sitting on this boat in Charleston, thinking that I was about fifteen years out of prison, we had paid every penny that I owed back, I had a good credit rating, owned a home in Maine, had a beautiful wife, my son was doing extremely well, and our conversations always ended with "I love you." I had a wild and crazy relationship with Jesus, who I now knew had been by my side the whole time, and I was finally free! That meant that I had surrendered to my addiction and had asked for help and received it. This was so overwhelming that from time to time, I would get on my knees on the boat and say, "Thank You, God, for saving a wretch like me."

If you have read this far, first of all, let me say thank you. Secondly, if you can relate and are struggling with addiction and everything that goes along with it, let me tell you, there is nothing that our God can't do. If you can't climb that mountain in front of you, then get your shovel because God will help you dig through it! I was so far past my dreams at this point that I can't even explain. I would drive up the dirt road to our house in Maine, and when I would come around the corner and see it, I would be in awe. I couldn't believe that it was ours. I had to pinch myself and thank God. I also knew in my heart that I had bigger things to do!

112 | A Fall to Grace

Chapter Eleven:
Blessings, Upon Blessings, Upon Blessings

He is wooing you from the jaws of distress to a
spacious place free from restriction, to the comfort
of your table laden with choice food.

Job 36:16

About two months into the hitch in Charleston, I got a call
asking if I wanted to take a survey boat out of Philly as a master
captain, which meant more pay, and getting into a division that I
really wanted to get into—working as a merchant mariner re-
quires flexibility and a willingness to make changes constantly.
So much for staying in Charleston! I did have to finish my hitch,
and Billy had planned on coming down to spend a few days with
me before I left. We had a great time, played golf, checked out
the downtown area, and ate all kinds of food. It was a great visit.
After he left, I packed all I could in my truck and headed back to
Cushing, ME.

My time at home was great, as always. We got a bunch of
lobsters and fresh crabmeat and enjoyed God's blessings. I ended
up going back to work early because they had shipped the boat
to a marina in Delaware City and really wanted it on the water
working as soon as possible. I had been told that it was all ready to
go, but when I saw the boat, that was quite far from the truth. The
boat was all in pieces and looked like nobody had taken care of
it, so I started putting things together and got two other captains
to work on it. It was not only going to survey but also run crew,

so that meant it was a twenty-four-hour boat and we would be rotating watches.

We were working on the Delaware River and working out of Chester, PA, so I knew the area well. The boat was slow, and doing crew runs was frustrating because it took so long. A couple of months after starting this job, Hurricane Florence hit the Carolinas, and it tore up the whole area around Charleston. There was major flooding, and our lease was coming to an end on the condo. Lori had to go back down, clean up the place, and move the rest of our stuff out. Because of the flooding, I-95 was closed, and she had to go on back roads through North and South Carolina. I was worried, but she is a farm girl, and she got it done, and we got our security deposit back. She made it home safe after a brief stop to visit me in Philly. I guess God was watching over us in that situation, also! Had we bought a property in Charleston, we may have had serious damage, or if I had chosen to stay on that job, I might have been there when the hurricane hit. Many times, we don't know why God does something, but He knows.

Billy called one day and said he and his girlfriend were going to sightsee in Philadelphia and asked if we could meet. It was such a surprise to see them all the way from DC. We had pizza in the parking lot where I was docked. He also came down, spent a couple of days with me that winter, and even went out on the boat with me! What a blessing!

Working on the river in Philly in the winter was not fun. At least in the last two years, the river had gotten iced in, meaning that the river had huge chunks of ice floating up and down the river, which could sink a small boat if we were hit. The Coast Guard would close parts of the river to traffic, and we would have to stay tied to the dock. It also snowed, and we would get freezing rain, so we would put salt on the deck and on the dock so people wouldn't slip and fall. I did not like the cold weather in Philly, and neither did Lori up in Maine. We were wondering why in the world did we move back up north?

114 | A Fall to Grace

The plan had been that when we were done with the Philly job, I would haul the boat out, get some work done to it, then bring the boat to Jacksonville, FL, and start working there. Well, in the dredging industry, things can change overnight, and I got a call that they were sending the boat to Texas and that I was to get it ready to go on a trailer to be transported. The problem was our union only covers us as far south as Alabama. Any further south, and we lose our union wages, so I had two choices: go with the boat and make half the usual pay or see where else they could send me. I decided on the latter, and they set me up with a job in Jacksonville, FL. I hauled the boat out and headed back to Maine, a little disappointed because I felt like the boat had been taken out from under me, but life goes on. The Jacksonville job was a long one, maybe three years, so as Lori and I were discussing it, we decided to start looking at places in Florida. As I started this new job, I was working on two boats. I would work two weeks on one and then two weeks on another and get two weeks off. Both boats were survey boats, so it was nice—no nights, just days.

I was staying at an extended-stay hotel, and as the job progressed, it looked like I would be there awhile, so Lori and I decided to sell the place in Maine and rent a house in Jacksonville until we found a place to buy in or around Charlotte County, FL. We had vacationed there previously, and we loved the Gulf Coast. We put the house up for sale, and in less than thirty-six hours, we had an offer over the asking price! We found a house to rent near Mayport, FL, really close to my work, with a nice backyard for our dog. So, off we went back to Florida!

There were a few reasons why we left Maine. The first was that I was feeling the pull to get back into lobstering, and history has proven I just can't stay clean doing it. The second was that we both had been really impacted by this church planting experience, and we had been really hurt by it. We weren't part of a church family, and we knew that was not healthy. We wanted to start fresh with God. The third was that my friends were all different and living

Chapter Eleven: Blessings, Upon Blessings, Upon Blessings | 115

their own lives. Once you are out of lobstering, you are out of mind, meaning they never came over to visit. We just needed a clean break to get back into our life of faith and to help others.

Before we moved, we started surrounding ourselves with positive Christian couples and found some really supportive people on the same path as us. We rented a U-Haul truck and a friend of ours, Glenn, helped pack it, and he drove it down to Jacksonville, FL, while we drove our car down. He got there a day after we arrived, so we unpacked, keeping most of it in the garage. The owners of the home let us use some of the furniture left in the house, so we had a couch, table, and a couple of chairs. I went back to work, and Lori made the house livable. We found a great church called Eleven22 with an awesome pastor, so the healing began.

We started making trips over to the Gulf Coast, around the Englewood area, and we fell in love with the place because it seemed more laid back compared to the East Coast of Florida. We rented an Airbnb in Englewood and started looking at houses in the area. The problem with some of the houses was they were between twelve to twenty years old and needed work. I just didn't feel confident telling if it was worth the money. We decided to look for land and build a place. This area of Florida had more of a sense of community, and the residents seemed to have many of the same values as us. The town we live in is on a large bay, perfect for fishing or just spending time on the water. God provided us with a wonderful place to live!

We traveled back and forth from Jacksonville to Port Charlotte for the next few months whenever I had time off. It was a four-hour trip one way, so it was a long haul. Things were going pretty full steam until COVID-19 hit, and it just slowed everything down to a crawl. We were supposed to get into the house around April, but that came and went, so we decided to move into an Airbnb in Englewood in the last few weeks to be closer to the house. I asked for a voluntary layoff for a few months so we could focus on the house. Building a house during a pandemic is terribly stressful! I've never really had much time off unless it was because of health issues or because I had been put in jail, so this was different. I'm sure my wife was getting upset with me because I was complaining about everything. I should have been dead years ago or in prison for life, but here I was, being ungrateful. God must have been just shaking His head.

Because of this slow, painful process, we were out of control with trying to micromanage the project. The poor project manager was trying his best, but I was calling him and being a jerk for really no reason, except the fact that I hadn't prayed before I called, so he was getting the old me. Florida construction crews are a little different than the ones in Maine. We would visit the building site, and there would be a crew working, but they would leave at 11 AM, and that was it for the day. Then they wouldn't show up for another three days. We had taken out a small construction loan, mostly so they would oversee the project and protect our financial interests. But even the bank was ultra-conservative. Let's put it this way, by the end of the build: I was so stressed out by the bank and delays in building that the only peace we had was in our church! We did find an awesome church called DC3 with another great pastor and started getting involved. We finally felt like we had found a church home again. Thank God for that!

We had started picking things up for the new house, so we were filling the Airbnb up with furniture. July had rolled around, and it was hot in SWFL. It looked like we were finally going to get to move in the middle of July, so we put out an SOS to Billy in DC, and he flew down to keep Lori and me from killing each other! Somehow, we got the garage code so that we could access our new home before closing, and we started filling up the garage. The builder did not want us to do this. I guess this is a prime example of people trying to do the godly walk but still being unruly sometimes! It just shows that we are real. In my mind, we had no ill intent; we were just desperate to move in. On July 8th, 2020, we finally signed the paperwork for the house, and I

Chapter Eleven: Blessings, Upon Blessings, Upon Blessings | 117

got to make good on another promise to my beautiful wife: that I would take care of her and that she wouldn't have to carry the load herself. This was the third house that I had purchased in seven years with my own credit. There is only one way that I could do this, walking by faith and guidance in Jesus Christ! Plus, my wife and son never lost hope in me.

Now it was time to go back to work, so I called the company, and they said to head to Charleston, SC, and split my time between two boats there. Off I went in the middle of a pandemic! I stopped at the dock and got my COVID-19 test, and then headed to Mount Pleasant to my hotel room. The two boats were survey boats, so I was just working days. That was great! We had a lot of equipment on this job, so we were very busy. The first hitch went like clockwork; I finished up the four weeks and headed home. It was an eight-hour drive. It was almost unreal to drive up to the new house. I was still in shock that we were able to do this. My wife greeted me at the door even though it was 1 AM and our dog, Leah, was going crazy! All was good in our lives. We went to church regularly and started meeting people. It felt like we were meant to be here. To shine the Light of Christ into others' lives.

Working with a Bucket Dredge

Chapter Eleven: Blessings, Upon Blessings, Upon Blessings | 119

Chapter Twelve: Grateful

The Lord is my Shepherd, I lack nothing. He makes me lie down in green pastures, He leads me beside quiet waters, He refreshes my soul. He guides me along right paths for His name's sake. Even though I walk through the darkest valley, I will fear no evil, for You are with me; Your rod and staff, they comfort me. You prepare a table before me in the presence of my enemies. You anoint my head with oil; my cup overflows. Surely Your goodness and love will follow me all the days of my life, and I will dwell in the house of the Lord forever.

Psalm 23

I started working up and down the Eastern Seaboard a little more, first to Cape Charles, VA, for two weeks and then to Staten Island, NY. The reason I was moving around so much was that I had asked my boss if I could start filling in whenever a captain was needed. This was the start of a new semi-retirement adventure. Cape Charles is a beautiful place because it is way down on the Delmarva Peninsula and quite secluded. As I was finishing up my two weeks, Hurricane Isaias came up the coast. On my last day, it came right over us. It had been downgraded to a tropical storm, but it still blew between forty to fifty knots. Luckily, it was moving quickly. I was staying in a motel off the beaten path with big pine trees everywhere, and when the storm passed, my truck was full of branches and pinecones! The storm was headed north, so I waited a little bit and followed it north to Staten Island. In my job, we are always dodging hurricanes and tropical storms, especially in the fall.

There were a bunch of tree limbs down and trees scattered all along the roads that I took to Staten Island. When I got to the hotel, the power was out, and they didn't know when it would be back on, so the company I worked for found me a hotel on the New Jersey side of Newark Bay. Driving around NYC wasn't really my cup of tea. Thank God for GPS because I wouldn't have been able to find our boatyard. In contrast, working at New York Harbor is so awesome. The Statue of Liberty and Manhattan are quite the sight. There is a lot of boat traffic, so you have to pay attention all the time and never let your guard down. I worked nights, so we would do our crew run, then tie up to a dock until 3–4 AM, then head to the yard and turn the boat over to the day captain. I finished my time there and headed home for my time off.

Next, I headed to Kings Bay, which is in Fernandina Beach, FL, where there is a submarine base. It was so interesting to see submarines and their support ships. We have an amazing naval force! Our company was deepening the channel. I was running a day boat working with one of our hopper ships. A hopper ship is a mobile dredge. It has an arm on each side that goes down to the bottom and acts like a big vacuum cleaner, sucking the sand onto the ship. The ship has a big hopper in the middle that fills up with material; then, either they bring it to a pump-out station and pump it onto a beach, or the ship takes the sand offshore and dumps it in a dumping area. The ship has doors on the bottom that open up and release the sand. It's quite an operation to watch them work, and we would bring their crew and supplies to them.

At the end of this trip, I got a call from Charleston, SC, and one of the captains wanted me to work with him on his boat, doing three weeks on and three weeks off. His wife was pregnant, and he wanted to spend as much time with her as he could. Talk about a God thing! I had been looking for a survey boat to do three weeks on and three weeks off, plus a good skipper to work with, and this job had all of the above!

During this time, COVID-19 was going strong. We were

122 | A Fall to Grace

considered essential workers, so we had special passes to cross state lines and work, even when the entire country was considered under quarantine. We would be sent home with a test kit, and a week before we were to report back for duty, we would take the test and send it in. We would hear back in two days whether we were negative or not. When we got to the boat, they would test us again. Nurses would also take our temperature every morning, so it was a pretty good system. We were expected to stay put when we were off duty. This was such a strange time in our country!

As I have said before, running out through Charleston Harbor was always so cool, with so much history on both sides. When we would get to the outer harbor, we would pass Fort Sumter and Fort Moultrie, where the first shots were fired to start the Civil War. I always imagined how much pain that war caused this great nation. Lori and I always visited a museum or two when she would come to visit me. Charleston had many rice plantations, which is something that I didn't know. We also loved to look at the historic houses and churches in Charleston.

The three weeks on and three weeks off schedule was really nice because after three weeks of straight work, I was ready to go home, and after three weeks off, I was ready to go back to work. We had two dredges onsite at first, which was okay, but as the job got busy, we ended up having two bucket dredges and, at one point, three hopper dredges. We also had contracted a hydraulic dredge from another company, so we were surveying for six dredges, which was a lot, to say the least! They finally rigged the other crew boat with multibeam survey equipment, so that really helped, but we were the offshore boat, so we did the bulk of the surveying. By late fall, we were surveying huge areas, and the weather was getting rough, so a few days a week, we would have to turn around at the jetties and head back.

Things had really changed due to COVID-19, but I was pretty healthy because I was taking supplements, eating right, and exercising. I believe that kept me COVID-free through all

Chapter Twelve: Grateful | 123

the traveling. Every once in a while, I had to jump over to the other crew/survey boats to work for a day or three because of COVID-19, but other than that, it was business as usual.

One interesting thing that happened that fall while I was working in Charleston was that a Netflix series called *Outer Banks* was filming on the dock next to ours for a few weeks. I never did see anyone from the show, but I did watch the show and could identify exactly where it was filmed.

Another time, I got a call from Billy saying he was in town doing a fundraiser for Senator Scott. We were able to meet up for dinner and hang out for a few hours. I am so proud of the man he has become and that he chose to follow his passion.

It's hard to be away from home all the time, so I bring my Bible with me and spend time in the Word in the morning before work. I also try to bring some God into everyone's lives, especially if they get onto any of the boats that I run. I don't push it, but I explain how God has saved a poor wretch like me. I also tell many people that I am clean and sober, which many just can't understand. I guess I never did either until a string of bad decisions and, ultimately, prison got my attention. I believe we can take ministry wherever we go!

During all this time, there has been so much division about COVID-19, vaccines, and politics. What really stinks about all this is that I have people I have known for fifty-plus years, and now they hate me for my beliefs. That's freaking crazy. I love everybody. I might not agree with you, but I'm still going to try and pull you up if you're drowning. I believe what is in the Bible. End of story. If you disagree, then that's okay; I still love you. I look at it this way, I have given my life to Jesus, and when I die, if there is no God, what have I lost? But if there is, and I believe there is, I have gained eternal life. Wow! That's a no-brainer for me. So, if you see me on a boat yelling and complaining about something, please know that I am human, and I fail every day. But I ask for forgiveness all the time, and Jesus gave His life for forgiveness.

While I was home this trip, my church had a men's group called Fight Club, so I signed up and went to the first meeting. It was a ten-week course that was physical, mental, and very spiritual. In the first meeting, we did a run in the rain and went through a small obstacle course. We had homework every Tuesday and had to complete it before the week's end. We were expected to do pushups and other physical activities daily, which motivated me to be in better shape. We read a book about having a father figure, which I never had as a boy, so it really spoke to me. I learned so much about myself in this group. I finished the course, and they had a nice graduation ceremony at our church, and a bunch of people showed up to support us. Lori was really proud that I participated and completed the program, which just made us closer.

I went back to work feeling positive and confident in my relationship with Jesus. It was late spring, and the weather was still nasty, so we got out when we could. We had one dredge offshore, so it was pretty easy. About ten days into this trip, I was offshore, and it was rough out with three-foot seas out of the northeast. I was doing a survey when a huge container ship passed us. Right behind it was the pilot boat, and I was rolling around trying to straighten our boat out, and I felt a pop and then another pop in my right shoulder. Then I got sick to my stomach and knew I had done something to my shoulder. I stopped the boat, stood up, and told the surveyor what had happened.

I called our safety officer on the way in and asked them to meet me at the dock. They took me to an emergency clinic, where they took X-rays and performed an MRI. I knew I had really messed my shoulder up. The doctor said that I had torn one tendon completely off, ripped two more tendons, and torn my bicep. I needed surgery to fix it. I headed home and was able to set up everything nearby. Both the company and the union were supportive, but it was a slow process for things to get done. They put me on painkillers, which I gave to my wife to dole out to me.

Chapter Twelve: Grateful | 125

That is what I have learned from past experiences, that I need to be proactive about my sobriety. The pain was intense, and I had a plan to get off the painkillers in five days, and that's what I did, but I wasn't happy about it.

I can say, without a doubt, that almost all bad things, if not all that happened to me, were a direct result of lawyers, drugs, and money. Not so much lawyers, but drugs and money are the tools of the devil. I had finally reached the point where I was putting God first, so this recovery was going to be drug-free! One of my favorite quotes goes like this, "A ship is safest in the harbor, but that's not what a ship is built for," and I believe that describes my life. God created me not to sit in a drug-induced haze but to go into this beautiful world and help people.

During my shoulder recovery, I had all this time on my hands, so I decided to call my cousin Kathy. I hadn't talked to her in years. Not sure why, but it had to be a God thing. As we talked, she started telling me that I had an uncle who lived about thirty miles south of me and that I had a whole bunch of cousins I never knew about. I had always suspected that my dad had other family, but he never said anything about them. I was curious, so I got the address and phone number, texted this person, and waited for a reply. It came a few days later, and he said he was my uncle and that I had three aunts and two uncles I had never met. I also had eight cousins, nineteen second cousins, and thirty-two third cousins. I was freaking out over this. I now had a family on my dad's side! It's just mind-blowing, and I can't wait to meet them all. I've had so many things happen to me over a lifetime, and this just made me feel really good!

I'm sitting here, writing this, looking out at the pool in a house we just had built, getting ready to head to a men's retreat called Marked Men for Christ, just feeling grateful. I often wonder how a low-down junkie with a prison record could have pulled himself out of that hole to be sitting here writing this today. I have two words, *God* and sobriety. It's the only reason that I am still alive! My heart has been changed forever.

I thank God for giving me the Breath of Life this morning. I just want to say to whoever needs to hear this: God loves you! There is no mountain too high or valley too low that He can't walk us through. If you are hurting, please hit your knees and ask for help. I am a testimony that it works. Find a church, find a recovery meeting, and get hooked up with some positive people. Start praying every morning and night. The power of the Holy Spirit will come upon you if you ask. There is nothing that you can't do with God, your Father. I implore you to try it. I have been down so many times, but not once have I ever thought that maybe I'd just stay down in the hole. No, I knew I had to move forward. Then I found the power of prayer, and that changed everything. It gave me a purpose. God has given me His grace. When I fall, He catches me in His hands. I never have to worry about getting up because through Him, anything is possible.

God bless, and I hope His grace finds you!

View from my office

Enjoying life